Report Writing in Business

The effective communication of information

T J Bentley

Viva Books Private Limited

New Delhi • Mumbai • Chennai • Kolkata • Bangalore • Hyderabad

Foreword

Report Writing in Business was first published in 1978, since when it has been reprinted numerous times both by CIMA and Kogan Page. This edition has been extensively rewritten and updated.

The book's message remains essentially the same: good reports present information in a clear, concise, readable way which gives a message without the danger of ambiguity or misrepresentation.

The book is aimed at business managers as well as students of management who need to write reports for consumption within their organisations. Many readers will, no doubt, be involved in writing, in part or in whole, reports intended for an external audience. The contents of many of these reports have their foundations in law, accounting standards and recommended practice. These reports are not covered in this book.

Report writing is an essential part of business life and those who can effectively communicate their ideas are likely to reap the rewards. Most managers and accountants use PCs (personal computers) that have report writing software, and grammar and spell checkers, together with readability indicators. However, many lack the essential, basic skills of report writing to make optimum use of the software – that is where this book is of use.

If having read this book, you feel you need more information on report writing, there is a wealth of material on the Internet that can easily be accessed.

Effective report writing: a checklist

- Always remember the readers. What are they looking for in your report?
- Keep the report as short and as simple as possible.
- Structure the report in the best way for the intended purpose. Plan your report to help you write it and to aid the reader's understanding.
- Include a succinct but accurate summary of your report and its key recommendations at the beginning.
- Thoroughly research and substantiate your information. Be sure of your facts.
- Avoid long sentences. Keep your writing to the point. Use the best words in the optimum order.
- Ensure that any graphics are correctly presented and labelled. Position them as close to the relevant text as possible.
- Check your report carefully. Read it aloud. Get someone else to read and critically appraise it. Don't be afraid to revise and improve it.
- Present your report attractively. Use technology to enhance not distract from your purpose. Use an indexing system that is easy for the reader to follow.
- Follow up your report with its recipients. Has it met their expectations? What course of action will they adopt as a result?

Introduction

A potential reader of a report has four questions:

1. What is the report all about?
2. Is it relevant to me?
3. Does it contain significant new information?
4. Should I read it now?

Every report writer has their own style. Reading this book will present you with the opportunity to use what you are learning to modify your own style and approach. Use those ideas that you feel will be most helpful towards improving your future reports.

The key to effective report writing is to be able to communicate your message in a way that enables readers to understand your message in exactly the way that you intend. To achieve this you need to be able to write with clarity, brevity and relevance. You need to be able to communicate your interest in, and enthusiasm for, your topic. You need to be able to engage and connect with your reader. You need to be persuasive and convincing.

This book is divided into three parts:

- Part 1 – Communicating effectively
- Part 2 – Writing reports
- Part 3 – Presenting facts and opinions.

The aim here is to provide your with a comprehensive, clear, brief and relevant set of guidelines for writing effective reports.

Part 1
Communicating Effectively

'Precision of communication is important, more important than ever, in our era of hair-trigger balances, when a false, or misunderstood word may create as much disaster as a sudden thoughtless act.'

James Thurber,
Friends, Romans, Countrymen Lend Me Your Ear Muffs, Lanterns and Lances

I talk and I write, but do I communicate?

The report writer must identify:

- the aim of writing;
- the audience;
- the reader's aim;
- the reader's background knowledge;
- what the reader needs to know;
- the reader's attitudes.

The overall aim is to produce a *simple message* that is easily understood and interpreted as you intend it to be. Always remember – keep it simple!

There are some basic skills that you need to use to achieve this aim and the purpose of this part is to explore what these are. This is done in three chapters:

1 Principles of good communication;
2 Signals and messages;
3 Barriers to communication.

1 Principles of Good Communication

The report writer's aim in communication is to pass a message to an individual or group that is understood and responded to in the way that you intend.

The means of achieving this aim is known as the communication process and consists of the following stages:

- **Purpose** – what you are trying to achieve.
- **Formation** – constructing the message in the most suitable form.
- **Transmission** – selecting the most appropriate means of passing your message to the audience.
- **Reception** – considering how the message will be received.
- **Perception** – determining the way the message will be interpreted.
- **Action** – deciding how to trigger the appropriate response and how to receive feedback on the response produced.

1.1 Purpose

All communication is a two-way process: it is the process of passing information effectively between individuals or groups. It requires firstly the report writer and secondly the recipient. You will create the message and transmit it to the recipient. The recipient will then interpret the message and, it is hoped, act accordingly.

It is important that you decide the response you want to obtain from the recipient before you start the communication process. What is the purpose of your message?

- To *inform* so that the recipient is fully aware.
- To *explain* so that the recipient completely understands.
- To *instruct* so that the recipient learns the correct techniques.
- To *advise* so that the recipient takes appropriate action.

- To *persuade* so that the recipient acts in agreement.
- To *sell* so that the recipient 'buys' and is not conscious of being 'sold'.
- To *discuss* so that the recipient agrees the basis of opinion or comment.
- To *question* so that the recipient provides relevant answers.

It is achieving the desired attitude and behaviour of the recipient which determines the success of the communication. It does not matter how much time and effort you put into the construction of the message and its transmission; if the recipient does not get the message and respond as expected, then you, as the communicator, have failed.

You must therefore ask and answer the following questions before proceeding:

- Who is your audience – the person or people for whom you are writing the report?
- What do they know already?
- What do they need to know?
- What do they want to know?
- How do you want them to respond?

It is your responsibility to ensure that the purpose is clear and that the communication process is carried through successfully.

1.2 Formation

Construction of the report in the most suitable form is impossible if you are not absolutely clear about the purpose. The message must be constructed so that the recipient interprets it in the way it is intended. It is much easier to tell people they are to receive a pay rise than to tell them they are redundant. Good news is easier to transmit and more readily received than bad news. But the way the message is constructed is not the only factor.

The reason for the communication obviously affects the content of the message and its structure. It might be a simple directive where one word will suffice, such as instructing a gun crew to 'fire', or a complex, lengthy explanation of the implications of a strategic decision on profit levels.

The choice of how to construct the message will depend upon your interpretation of the recipient's 'wave length'. The way the recipient will best be able to receive and interpret the information contained in the message is fundamental to the way it is constructed.

Messages commonly consist of a mixture of:

- words;
- numbers;
- symbols;
- drawings and diagrams;
- photographs.

When the communication involves presentations you also have to consider delivery style, body language and gestures.

All these must be used with care so that the message is clear and unambiguous when it is received.

1.3 Transmission

The transmission process involves choosing the most appropriate way to get the message from your mind into the mind of the recipient, so that both of you interpret the message in the same way. This choice will depend upon the circumstances and these may not always enable you to choose an approach that ideally you would like. This can immediately create a barrier to successful communication but the problem can be alleviated, to some extent, if you are prepared to be flexible in your approach and attitude.

The choice of the most appropriate method will depend upon factors such as time, distance and impact, as well as the purpose, the circumstances, the mechanics available and, of course, you and the recipient

1.4 Reception

For communication to work the recipient must 'get the message', understand it, interpret its meaning correctly and act accordingly. For this to happen not only must the message be constructed properly and delivered in the best possible way it must also arrive at a time and place, and in suitable conditions, so that the recipient is willing and prepared to receive it.

You will succeed in getting your message across if you make sure, as far as possible, that it arrives at an appropriate time. This is much easier to state than it is to do, but a little effort in preparing the ground is usually well worthwhile.

Managing expectations is important and you should consider:

- briefing recipients on your progress at regular intervals;
- gaining an understanding of your recipient's work commitments so that your message will be received at the best time for it to be read, understood and actioned.

Such simple approaches can make an enormous difference.

1.5 Perception

Perception is the process of receiving, recognising and interpreting signals so as to gain awareness of their meaning and implications. It is obvious that this must take place in the mind of the recipient before any communication can take place.

There are three key words in the first part of this definition:

1. receiving;
2. recognising;
3. interpreting.

First, the message must reach the recipient's mind and senses. Second, the signals received must be recognised and should be known and identifiable. Third, the signals must be linked in such a way that the recipient's mind can interpret a meaning from them.

The brain receives visual images and sounds, and checks them against a library of images and sounds previously developed from education, training and life experience. If there is an exact or similar image or sound on file the brain checks the meaning or meanings already stored and relates them to the circumstances. If there is a match or near match, the brain assigns an interpretation to the signals and, if necessary, acts accordingly.

You can help this process to work by using words, images and sounds that are likely to be in the recipient's mental library and have the desired meaning already attached to them. In this way, the recipient's brain will be able to create a suitable match and apply an appropriate meaning.

Always view your communication from the point of view of the intended recipient. Once the meaning has been derived the recipient can determine the implications and make the appropriate response.

1.6 Action

The final part of the communication process is for the recipient to respond as desired. This may be a very direct, simple action or a more complex series of actions.

The response to the directive 'fire' would be the pressing of a button to activate the firing mechanism. The communication process can be seen quite clearly in Figure 1.1.

Figure 1.1: The communication process

Purpose	*To get the gunner to fire the gun.*
Formation	*The word 'fire'.*
Transmission	*The word 'fire' is shouted within hearing of the gunner.*
Reception	*The gunner hears the word 'fire'.*
Perception	*The word 'fire' is regonised and means, in this context, 'press the firing mechanism'.*
Action	*The gunner presses the firing mechanism.*

1.7 Barriers to communication

The communication process, simply described above, has to overcome many barriers, most of which are created by the people involved. The main problems encountered are dealt with in Chapter 3, but for the moment we will record the fact that good communicators recognise that barriers exist and take the responsibility for overcoming them.

Remember: make it as easy as possible for the recipient to 'get the message'.

2 Signals and Messages

Humans have always used their senses to receive signals to warn of danger. The principal senses humans use for communication are those of sight and sound, which allow signals to be transmitted over long distances. For signals to be effective as a method of communication they must be easily recognised and interpreted. Signals warning of danger must be sufficiently obvious to draw the recipient's attention to them. Bright colours and loud noises are examples of simple and effective signals.

By linking signals together in sequence, complex messages can be transmitted. Native drums and smoke signals are early examples of using sequences of signals in this way. Later, flags and Morse code were used.

Modern communication is still based on the concept of signals directed at the human senses, but these signals now take many different forms, including words, numbers, symbols, drawings and diagrams, style, body language, gesture and sounds. When arranged in appropriate sequences these signals provide the basis for messages ranging from the very simple warning sirens to complex multimedia presentations, reinforcing subtle messages.

One of the primary skills in communication is that of being able to arrange signals in the most effective way to make the resultant message intelligible to the recipient.

2.1 Words

Words are the basic element of language. When linked together in a prescribed way they provide a means of describing, explaining and expressing an unlimited range of emotions, feelings, expressions, etc. Sentences are constructed by the rules of grammar.

Grammar is a systematic description of the way a language works. It describes the individual words that occur in a language, the forms they take and the ways speakers and writers put them together in meaningful combinations.

An individual word has a certain meaning which is held in the brain, alongside the library of sounds that are recognised as that particular word. Let us take two words in order to see how this works. Consider the words 'blue' and 'sky'. Each has a particular meaning in the mind. When we link words together the meaning is adapted depending on the order of the words we use. 'Blue sky' means something different from 'sky blue'.

As we increase the number of words in the combination, so we can extend and adapt our meaning. If we also consider the inflexion we put on words then the scope is enormous, for example:

'Lancashire are playing cricket'

has quite a different meaning from

'Are Lancashire playing cricket?'

To use words effectively it is necessary to know how to put them together in simple, easy-to-understand combinations. The basic combination of words is the sentence. In report writing long sentences should be avoided. Complicated information should be communicated in short sentences or bullet points. The sentence length should be flexible to add to readibility and avoid the 'boredom factor'.

Sentences are usually grouped in paragraphs that have a common theme and in this way aid the structure of the report.

2.2 Graphical communication

Graphical communication comprises:

- numbers;
- symbols;
- pictures:
  - graphs (e.g. line or bar) and charts (e.g. pie);
  - drawings;
  - diagrams;
  - photographs.

Using these alone or in combination can communicate more information per square centimetre than the same amount of text. When using these aids ensure that they are also clearly explained in the text.

2.2.1 Numbers

Numbers are special symbols for words that describe quantities They are a form of shorthand that makes the manipulation of quantities easier. The use of spreadsheet software means that it is common for numbers to be presented in columns or rows, or in the form of mathematical notation.

There are three golden rules for communicating using numbers:

1. ***Significance***

   As a rule, remove the insignificant many and concentrate on the significant few. Aim to have no more than four figures across the column. In accounting reports, for example, if the figures are in millions then it is appropriate to round them to the nearest thousand.

2. ***Order***

   Numbers should be presented in the order which matches the recipient's interest rather than in strict logical order. It is usual for the most interesting numbers to appear at the bottom right-hand corner of many accounting reports. This is because convention and mathematical logic dictates this approach. The approach can be improved by preceding the table with a sentence such as: 'In the following table there is an adverse contribution variance of £345,000 which is 20% of the budget. This is due to a lower level of sales (£615,000 less than budget), only partially offset by favourable direct cost variances of £270,000.' This sentence directs attention to the most important numbers and guides the reader's examination of the figures.

3. **Layout**

   Use plenty of space and dividing lines to punctuate numbers so that the eye can make sense of them.

2.2.2 Symbols

Symbols overcome the problem of different languages and are more easily learned than the relevant words. They can be extremely effective when used imaginatively for communication of information, particularly when used in conjunction with graphical presentation. Symbols enable fast, meaningful recognition to take place, as long as the recipient's brain can recognise, if not fully then substantially, the symbols presented.

Symbols can also replace groups of words with simple visual signals, as in these examples:

In words	*Symbolically*
Three (is less than) five	$3<5$
This (is equal to) that	this = that
X (is more than) *Y*	$X>Y$

2.2.3 Pictures

According to the Chinese proverb: 'A picture is worth a thousand words.' But this is true only if the picture describes what is wanted and if the recipient is able to give the desired meaning to the visual message. The eye is a very accurate receiver of images. However, it is still necessary for the brain to check its files and ascribe a meaning to the visual signals received. The brain can be tricked because it imposes its own interpretation on what the eye perceives and if the image turns out to be a confused visual image the brain will be confused or will place a wrong interpretation on the image.

Appropriate visual images can have a powerful impact and can be much better than words at communicating particular messages. Numerical information can easily be converted into graphs using spreadsheet packages but again it is important for these to add to communication not distract from it. Photographs too can be used, for example in annual reports or on web pages.

2.3 Body language

It is usual for report writers to give presentations of their report. Presentation software such as Powerpoint helps in the construction of slides but presenters must always be aware of the 'messages' they are conveying through their body language.

Body language is usually very meaningful, once a person has learned how to interpret the signals. It has been estimated that over 75% of communication is through body language. Frowns, raised eyebrows, a smile, a shrug of the shoulders, nervous tapping of the fingers, the slight nod or shake of the head, all convey a particular meaning within the context of what is happening at the time the gesture is made.

The use of hands can become a language in itself, for example the sign language used by the deaf and the language used on the racecourse by the tic-tac men. The use of gestures must not be underestimated as a means of communication. When linked with the spoken word, gestures can change the whole meaning of what is being said.

2.4 Sounds

Words, when spoken, are sounds that we have come to receive and understand in a certain way. Through the process of learning a language we learn to recognise sounds and associate a meaning with them. When we first learn to read we do so by converting the symbols we see into sounds which we recognise through association with visual images presented at the same time. Gradually, we associate the symbols directly with the visual images without having to make the sounds. However, many people still follow the same procedure in the brain: they see the symbol, they associate it with a sound, and then they give the sound a meaning.

Sounds and visual images are the primary records within the brain that we use for communication. However, the association of our other senses with sounds and images provides us with a very sophisticated repertoire of devices to promote effective understanding.

2.5 Signs

When used in combination with the written and spoken word other communication tools such as signs and the use of colour can greatly add to the recipient's understanding of the message. They can also attract and keep the audience's interest.

Multi-media presentations, when properly structured and combining the spoken word, slides, video, music, printed materials, or inviting audience interaction, are an extremely effective way to communicate a wide range of messages. They engage all the senses of the audience. Be careful though, overuse of any visual medium will reduce its impact and eventually lose the audience's interest.

Don't go overboard when using technology. Remember to use the tools available to add to the impact of your report not distract from it. Technology will not make a bad report good but when used properly can dramatically increase its impact.

The same rules of communication apply to presentations:

- Use bullet points and restrict the number of points per slide to no more than six.
- Restrict the number of slides to those necessary to cover the key points of the report.
- Restrict the length of time of your presentation to keep the attention of the audience. Depending on the content, a presentation may last, say, 20 minutes and can be followed by an open questions and answers session.

3 Barriers to Communication

There are eight main barriers that need to be overcome if communication is to be effective. These are:

1. language;
2. vocabulary;
3. class;
4. attitude;
5. position;
6. personality and character;
7. mood;
8. knowledge of subject.

3.1 Language

It is obvious that if we do not speak the same language we are going to fail to communicate effectively. In some circumstances, gestures (sign language) can achieve limited success. If we are transmitting information we should take care to see that our audience does at least understand the same language. A message will be far more effective if it is sent in the language used by the recipients. It should not be assumed that they will take the trouble to translate something they cannot understand. In an era of increasing globalisation the need to be able to communicate in many different languages is increasingly important.

Getting reports translated into different languages is not easy. There are many translation agencies that offer services but it is important to get a translation that not only uses the correct words but also conveys the meaning behind them. In a multinational organisation, getting someone to prepare the translation may be relatively easy. Such translators are likely to be employed locally and will thus have the necessary language and associated customs/conventions knowledge. Smaller organisations that are serious about their overseas business are likely to have agents who can signpost translation agencies and who may be prepared to assist in the translation itself.

3.2 Vocabulary

The predilection to perpetrate incomprehensible formulations of loquacious 'literary expressions should be strenuously discouraged by those responsible for the dissemination of information'. In other words use of big words should be avoided by communicators.

Whenever we prepare a message of any kind we should remember that the vocabulary of most people is limited. Proving that yours is not does little to assist the communication process. There is no greater compliment for speakers or writers than to be told that what they have written or said is accessible and understandable.

Avoid attempting to be too clever. Choose the right words, avoid emotive words, and don't be overly formal. Use the best words in the best order.

3.3 Class

Class is often a fundamental barrier to effective communication. It is not only the language and the words used that are important, but also the way we use them, and this is mainly determined by our social background and environment. There are many advertisements asking for people who are able 'to communicate with all levels of management'. It requires considerable tact and understanding to do this effectively. Don't be pompous, especially when communicating with subordinates.

3.4 Attitude

A recipient's attitude can be determined by the approach you use. The way we address a recipient should depend on the content of the message.

Body language can trigger 'guard' or 'relax' mechanisms in a recipient. It requires a very clever person to deliver a message of rebuke without disturbing the recipient's attitude. There are few people who can deliver such messages with poise, charm and tact, but nevertheless it is possible.

3.5 Position

Perhaps one of the most difficult communication problems with people stems from the direction of the communication. There is no doubt that people communicate differently with their bosses, their staff and their colleagues, not only in the way they transmit their messages, but also in the attention which they give to them. However, with a properly constructed and persuasive report, and 'expectation management', this problem can be minimised.

3.6 Personality and character

No matter how hard we try there are some people with whom we just cannot reach an understanding. We are all individuals, with our own personalities and characters, and this determines how we are treated by others. Some characteristics impinge directly on our ability to communicate effectively.

It is not easy to change personalities but attitudes can be altered. We should start by examining our own attitudes and personality, and gauge the effect we have on other people. We must find ways of minimising the adverse impact upon our communications of things in our make-up that we cannot change. It is rightly said that we are unaware of our impact on others until we see ourselves on video, with sound, and realise how many irritating habits we have.

3.7 Mood

The old saying 'There's a time and place for everything', is particularly true of communication. Said at the wrong time and in the wrong place, the simplest of words can cause chaos. A good communicator tests the mood and responds to it. Moods may be created by an individual or by groups. Responding to the current mood is important if we are to communicate effectively. If you cannot judge the atmosphere you will fail to choose the right moment to pass on your message, and in so doing fail to communicate.

3.8 Subject knowledge

It is important, of course, to have an adequate knowledge of the subject you need to communicate, but this can also be a danger. One thing that should be established is whether the recipient's knowledge is greater than yours, or vice versa. To show appreciation for another's knowledge helps break down the communication barriers. It also helps you to pitch your report at the right level. If you underestimate a person's knowledge you may include too much detail for someone who already knows a lot about the subject. They may become bored and skip through the report, missing important points unknowingly. On the other hand, too little information for someone unfamiliar with the topic won't help them to understand the issues.

It is fair to suggest that the 'human problems' in communication are the major ones. E-mail can certainly make communications faster and spread the message further, but the basic 'human problems' still need to be overcome. Knowing when to use short e-mail messages for example, or longer, more formal approaches or attachments, can be crucial to the way your communication is received and acted upon.

3.9 You, the transmitter

All the considerations outlined above also apply, in reverse, to you – the transmitter. You must also identify within yourself exactly the same problems as those experienced by the recipient. If you do not speak the same language as the recipient then it is your duty to translate the message into the recipient's language before transmitting it.

If you know the recipient you can pitch the vocabulary used at the correct level. If you don't know your target audience then observe caution and keep the vocabulary simple. At all costs, class bias should be removed from communication wherever possible, if only for the sake of good manners and respect.

You set the tone of the communication. The attitude set will be decided by the intentions of the message. Like attitude, your position or status has a bearing on communication. There are few people who are aggressive to those above them without first finding just cause, but obviously it is easy to be aggressive to subordinates. There is a direct relationship between attitude and position.

Personality and character can be adapted to suit the needs of the recipient, depending on the recipient's knowledge of the transmitter. It is a question of body chemistry. A good relationship usually ensures good communication. A poor relationship can have the opposite result. Adapting to the mind of the intended recipient is a difficult skill to master and use correctly, but it can be learned.

Your mood can upset or enhance that of the recipient's. Communication can be set on a simple scale: a good mood results in good communication; a bad mood, in bad communication. Remember, mood is a two-way process—and both parties can, accidentally or otherwise, reinforce or defuse it.

Good transmitters will put themselves in the place of the recipient. Good recipients will put themselves in the place of the transmitter. The ability to do this will increase the measure of understanding experienced by each party.

3.10 Communication needs

Our individual communication needs, both as transmitters and recipients, vary considerably. They depend upon:

- the job we do;
- the size of the organisation;
- the geographical spread of the organisation;
- the way activities are organised;
- the style of management.

Each individual will have to assess their own needs and act accordingly.

Part 2
Writing Reports

❛ Writing has laws of perspective, of light and shade, just as painting does, or music. If you are born knowing them fine. If not learn them. Then re-arrange the rules to suit yourself. ❜

Truman Capote (Interview),
Writers at Work, First series

Written reports are perhaps the most frequently used method of presenting information for management. Reports are written by most accountants and managers and cover a wide range of topics.

The aim of any report should be clear. Is it to pass on information, to persuade someone to take a particular course of action, to answer a question, to ask a question, to give instructions, or simply to give pleasure? The aim is crucial as it affects the content and the format.

Every piece of writing should have a purpose. It is effective only if it achieves that purpose. It will not achieve the purpose if the reader does not read it. There is no way you can make someone read what you have written. People must be encouraged at least to pick it up and start reading. From then on it's up to you.

4 Objectives of Report Writing

Before putting pen to paper or fingers to keyboard you should ask yourself: 'Why am I writing this report?' There are many apparent answers ranging from: 'Because I have been asked to,' to 'I don't know. '

The only valid answer to the question must consist of a specific objective. No report should be written without a clearly defined objective. There are four principal reasons for writing reports but each report, regardless of type, will have its own specific objective. If this is not clear to you then there is little if any hope of the report being effective. The four principal reasons for writing reports are:

1. to obtain agreement to a course of action – persuasive;
2. to explain specific events – explanatory;
3. as a basis for discussion – discussive;
4. to inform – informative.

4.1 Persuasive reports

The aim is clearly to persuade the reader to a particular point of view. This is never a simple process. It is necessary to write clearly and concisely and to present arguments in such a way that the reader fully understands your thoughts and the processes leading to the recommendations. You cannot report all the data and information which you have collected as a result of the work you have done. You must therefore be able to summarise the information in a form which allows for a full appreciation of the subject matter.

To obtain agreement you must write your report in a particular way that persuades the reader to accept your recommendations. This calls for a special approach and a structure which helps to achieve this.

4.2 Explanatory reports

Many reports are written for the sole purpose of explaining certain events. These can vary from complex reports of major disasters to simple reports on customer complaints. This type of report calls for an approach which clearly sets out the facts and can be seen by the reader to be unbiased, fully explaining the event under review.

4.3 Discussive reports

Discussions can be significantly improved if there is a written basis for the discussion. Reports for discussion purposes are often referred to as 'papers'. Regardless of the name given to the document they form a special type of report which requires a particular approach.

4.4 Informative reports

An informative report increases the reader's knowledge. It tells them something they did not already know, or places an interpretation on known facts which they had not considered. One of the most common informative reports is the 'progress' report, the aim of which is to bring the reader up to date on a specific subject.

The type of report being written will, of course, determine the methods used. The objectives you wish to achieve will determine the exact form and the content you use. Before starting work on a report you should ask yourself the following three questions in the order given here:

1. Why am I writing this report?
2. Which type of report should it be?
3. What are the specific objectives I hope to achieve?

Only when clear meaningful answers are available should you begin the report writing process.

4.5 The audience

The audience you are trying to reach via your writing will affect the language you use, the length of the piece, the format of the work and the style. Jargon should be avoided at all costs. Think about what the audience will understand. If you have to use technical terms explain them when they are first introduced. Expand abbreviations at least once. Try as far as possible to avoid jargon – the unnecessary use of technical terms. It is as refreshing to read jargon-free writing as it is to hear jargon-free speech.

Similarly, with humour. Humour can make a difficult subject easier to understand but equally it can get in the way of the subject. Remember, your sense of humour may not be the same as the reader's so use it with caution.

Your audience may be trained in receiving, reading and understanding reports; on the other hand they may not. The method of presentation should allow for this difference in ability. Readers should not be expected to ascend to your literary level. They won't, so don't attempt to make them.

Keep the language simple. Check you have done this by calculating the Fogg index. Take a sample piece of writing (100 words, say). Calculate the average words per sentence. Count the number of words with three or more syllables (except capitalised words, combinations and words ending in -ed or -es). Add the two numbers together and multiply by 0.4. The readability score is measured as follows:

- 5 fairly easy;
- 7–8 standard;
- 9–11 fairly difficult;
- 12–15 difficult;
- 17+ very difficult.

Deciding on the length of the written work is important. If it is too short you fail to get the message across; too long and you lose your reader. Finding a balance is not easy. One method that can be used is to write the piece then try to reduce every paragraph by at least one sentence. Good editing is important and with frequent practice it becomes less a process of mutilation and more a process of amendment.

Choosing the most appropriate format depends again on who it is for. Some individuals like to receive correspondence and reports in a certain form. If so, use that form. If the choice is yours, think about the people concerned, the time they will have to read it, and how involved and interested they are.

Style comes with experience. Let it happen naturally. Attempting to develop a style will lead to an unnatural flow. Start by writing what you want, how you want, and take it from there.

4.6 Content

Many people feel that the content is a constraint on how they write. It should not affect how you write, only the form that you use. In later chapters the handling of certain specific content is dealt with. For the moment, it will suffice to say that you decide the content once the objective has been established.

Written presentation in all its forms is a powerful communication device if used properly. Unfortunately many people do not give it the attention it deserves and consequently many desks are piled high with unwanted, unreadable paperwork.

4.7 The method

The aim of this book is to provide an insight into the methods of effective report writing. Knowing what you want to say, to whom and the reason, is of no avail if you cannot say it effectively.

4.8 Readability

Readability is one key to successful writing. People must find the text easy to read and interesting. Readability can be achieved if the following simple rules are used:

- Ensure you start on a high point of interest. The title must catch the reader's attention in much the same way as a headline in a newspaper.
- Other points of interest must be introduced approximately every 500 words. This will of course depend upon the text but in report writing 500 words gives plenty of time for the previous point to sink in.
- Avoid the passive voice and use the active voice. Using 'you' and 'we' makes the reader empathise with your text.
- Avoid using mathematical formulae or detailed statistical tables in the main body of the report.
- Avoid impersonal writing but at the same time avoid bias.
- Finish on a high point with a positive or firm conclusion.

The need to consider the reader's interest is vital if you wish to get your message across.

5 The Approach

5.1 The basic rules

The basic rules of report writing are:

- **Brevity** – If you can say what you want to say in a dozen words do not write 200. Thin reports are attractive, easy to handle, cheap to reproduce, easy to change and usually much more readable. Nobody complains of a report being too short.
- **Simplicity** – A report is a means of communication; it is not the place to prove your technical knowledge or your command of the English language. Only use words that everyone will be able to read and understand.
- **Purpose** – Remember why you are writing the report and try to put yourself in your reader's shoes. It is all too easy to get lost in your writing. We all review our own writing as writers, not as readers, and consequently we often hide the message amongst too many words.
- **Begin** – Have a meaningful beginning which explains the reason for the report and introduces the reader to the subject. If readers are aware of the report's history and the basic subject matter they can always skip the beginning.
- **End** – Always end by summarising how the report has achieved its objectives. You don't need to actually write 'the end' but readers should be quite clear that they have reached the end.
- **Content** – Make sure that the main content of the report is readable with points of interest well spaced throughout the report.
- **Title** – Give the report a meaningful name.
- **Author** – Always name the writer or writers.
- **Date** – Always date the report.

The above basic rules should always be applied. If you consider them to be commonsense then we are part of the way to achieving the aims of this book. All too often these basic rules, whether commonsense or not, are ignored and the results can be found in the files of any organisation.

5.2 The basic rules

Before going on to look at some of the key components of the different types of report, a quick word on getting started.

There is nothing more off-putting than a blank sheet of paper. The most difficult part of report writing can be getting started in the first place. This may be due to the difficulties in getting organised. To overcome this:

- plan the layout of your report;
- plan the layout of each section; and then
- start writing.

Plans make it easier to get started. They also provide a framework for the document and help you get organised. Plans may be in sentences, words or diagrams.

The early sections of your writing may be stilted until you get into the full flow. Don't worry – at least you have something to work with and it can always be edited or re-written later.

5.3 Persuasive reports

(See Example 1 on page 81.)

Reports written to obtain agreement should convince the reader of the validity of the arguments as the report proceeds. To do this it is vital to approach the report in a specific way. The introduction should be followed immediately by a summary of the main recommendations. This method, referred to by many people as starting at the end, is used for a very practical reason. If readers know from the beginning what the conclusions are, they will read the report in a particular way. They will be looking for the facts and arguments that support the recommendations. If they are doing this then they are more likely to find the recommendations than if you leave them to read the report and develop their own conclusions.

The report is not a thriller – you are not trying to spring any surprises at the end or trick the reader. You are trying to convince readers that a particular course of action should be followed. By concentrating their minds from the outset on this point you have a far greater chance of succeeding. To be effective, this approach must be followed with care and understanding. It will take time and practice to become adept at writing this type of report.

The guidelines given here should be an aid in organising the layout of a persuasive report:

- title page containing the date, the subject matter and the distribution of the report;
- an introduction to the subject matter – the survey which is the basis of the report;
- a summary of recommendations;
- a summary of the present position;
- scope of the survey;
- observations on recommendations;
- conclusion;
- appendices.

5.3.1 Introduction

The introduction should detail the reason why the survey has been carried out, who asked for the survey to be done and the ultimate aim.

5.3.2 Summary of recommendations

Each recommendation should be written briefly and clearly so that there is no doubt whatsoever about the recommendation being made. The recommendation should be short and simply state facts. Use bold type to add emphasis.

The following are examples of concise recommendations:

- that a computer network be introduced;
- that the following systems are processed on the new computer – sales, purchases, accounts and payroll;
- that the number of staff in the accounts department be reduced;
- that the new computer network be introduced within six months;
- that the wages, cashiers, purchase, sales and invoicing departments be amalgamated.

The aim of summarising recommendations is to enable the reader to obtain a ready grasp of the subject matter and to read the remainder of the report on the basis of justifying the recommendations.

Taken together the introduction and the summary of recommendations make up the 'executive summary' that many people include in reports.

5.3.3 Summary of present position

You should write this as briefly as possible indicating the salient points and the problems which were found to exist. Putting this in the report enables the reader to focus on the reasons for the survey and the recommendations.

5.3.4 Scope of the survey

This is the section in which you should describe clearly the work in the survey to enable the reader to see that the recommendations have been made after due consideration. Again, this should be a fairly brief section showing what work has been done and the timetable followed.

5.3.5 Observation on recommendations

In this section, each recommendation and the reason for it is dealt with separately and fully, and a considerable amount of time should be spent on it. This section should form the basis of the arguments for and against each recommendation. You could do this by producing a balance sheet with two columns headed 'pros' and 'cons'.

Each observation should repeat the recommendation and, wherever possible, indicate that the recommendation has been arrived at with the agreement of those affected by its implications. This is perhaps the most important section of the report and provides the opportunity for you to present a clearly argued case for the recommendations.

5.3.6 Conclusion

This section should be a short and unambiguous statement of your conclusions and provide the reader with a clear understanding of any future action that must be taken.

5.3.7 Appendices

Appendices are extremely useful in removing detailed statistics, tables, documents, etc., from the body of the report. If this is done, the body of the report will be much more readable, but there should be a simple cross reference in the text to the relevant parts of the appendices. The need for appendices depends on the length and complexity of the report. If the report is brief, then appendices will not be required; if it is complex then appendices can be used effectively.

If the reader finishes the report and is not in complete agreement, do not be surprised. What you are trying to achieve is basic agreement and an understanding of the content. There will always be a number of points that are queried. If the reader comments, 'Well on the whole I agree with your findings, but I have one or two questions,' then you can be justifiably pleased with your efforts.

5.4 Explanatory reports

(See Example 2 on page 86.)

Reports which set out to explain some event or situation, must be written in an unbiased way. They must be factual statements that do not lead the reader to arriving at a particular conclusion. For this reason they demand an approach almost the exact opposite to that of the persuasive report.

The twin enemies of the explanatory report are ambiguity and contradiction. These can largely be overcome by following the sequence indicated below:

- title, author and date;
- introduction:
- persons/departments involved;
- sequence of events;
- action taken;
- cause and effect;
- conclusion.

5.4.1 Title

In this type of report it is important to state clearly the subject being explained. This is often done with a main title and a subtitle.

5.4.2 Introduction

In this case, the introduction should cover two main points:

1. the reason for the report and who requested it;
2. the position and authority of the author.

This should be done in such a way that the reader has a pen picture of the subject.

5.4.3 Persons involved

An explanatory report is almost always about people. It is important, therefore, that if titles are used they are clear and unambiguous, and if names are used it must be clear who the people are and the positions they hold.

5.4.4 Sequence of events

This is an historical analysis of the sequence of events from the beginning to the end of the subject being examined. No comment is made in this section on the specific actions or their causes. It should be a simple, straightforward record of what happened.

5.4.5 Action taken

This section deals with every action, or the critical ones, in the same sequence as the historical analysis and sets out the reasons for the action. Where action was based on specific pieces of information these should be included as appendices. This section is the crux of the report.

5.4.6 Cause and effect

Taking each act in sequence, the results are analysed as to the cause and effect. This is the section where you might find difficulty in remaining unbiased. It is very difficult not to add your own interpretation of causes and care must be taken to remain factual.

In most events which require explanation something is done at the end. This may correct problems, be disciplinary or even be an attempt to cover up the problem altogether. It is important to analyse these subsequent actions as these may change the reader's view of the whole incident.

5.4.7 Conclusion

The final section should state how the information has been gathered, how long it has taken and the accuracy of the content. Any missing evidence should be noted and comments made on its importance. You should not draw your own conclusions or recommend action unless you have been asked to do so.

The important job of fact finding and marshalling content is dealt with in Chapter 6: it is a vital part of writing an explanatory report.

5.5 Discussive reports

(See Example 3 on page 94.)

Discussion without a report has a marked disadvantage: it is potentially lacking in purpose and focus. It is not always possible in conversation to make the same logical and forceful points which can be placed in a report. The spoken word is of great value in emphasising particular aspects, but statistics cannot be effectively considered nor can the full effect of a complex topic be appreciated only by listening. It has been said that two-thirds of what one hears is not registered by the brain.

To aid the discussion the report should not be written specifically to persuade or purely to explain. It is mainly a factual document but must allow sufficient latitude for discussion. Like the other types of report the discussive report has an aim and so must be properly organised. The approach which experience has proved effective is as follows:

- title, author and date;
- introduction;
- scope of the subject;
- discussion points;
- possible action;
- conclusion.

5.5.1 Introduction

This should state clearly that the report has been written as a basis for discussion and indicate the subject to be discussed. It is often useful to include here a note on how the report came to be written, who asked for it and why.

5.5.2 Scope of the subject

It is important for the reader to be able to identify quite clearly what the subject is and the boundaries of the discussion. This section must set the scene for the discussion and should enable the chairman of the meeting to control the discussion within the boundaries indicated. The source of the content should be set down together with a note of the methods used to collect the information.

5.5.3 Discussion points

Written in a number of ways, this section sets out the main points for discussion. It is helpful to the reader if each point is made and then the reason for discussing it given. Sufficient information must be provided for the reader to be able to comment on it in the discussion. People can and very often do stall at taking action through lack of information. Comments such as 'I need more information before I can comment,' are heard regularly. You should make sure that this is *not* the reaction to your reports.

5.5.4 Possible action

We normally expect some outcome from a discussion. In order for those taking part to have some idea of the outcome it is important to provide an indication of possible action that could be taken.

5.5.5 Conclusion

The conclusion should summarise the reason for the discussion and what it is hoped can be achieved by action stemming from the meeting. This will give purpose to the discussion and make people feel that it is worthwhile attending and commenting.

5.6 Informative reports

(See Example 4 on page 101.)

An informative report is written, as its name suggests, primarily to give information. It is intended to increase the reader's knowledge about a specific event or possibly to bring the reader up to date. There is often a significant overlap between explanatory and informative reports. By its very nature an explanatory report is informative. The informative report is more general and is approached somewhat differently.

The main sections are:

- title, author and date;
- introduction ;
- plan;
- body of the report;
- conclusion.

5.6.1 Introduction

This should state what the report is for, the reason for writing it and what it is hoped will be achieved.

5.6.2 Plan

This section can sometimes be incorporated in the introduction. In informative reports, the plan is very important because different readers may be more or less interested in different sections. The information in the report may cover a wide area, but there must always be a reason for including it. The plan clearly shows how each part of the report fits together.

5.6.3 Body of the report

There are a number of ways the body of the report may be organised. The most effective is to produce a number of sub-sections each of which deals with one main piece of information. Care must be taken to see that each sub-section relates to the others. There must be an overall theme. The aim is to increase the reader's knowledge. This will not be achieved if the reader has to jump from one subject to another.

5.6.4 Conclusion

Normally the conclusion of an informative report should state the reason why the report has been written and what, if anything, it is hoped will happen next.

5.7 Flexibility of approach

Each of these four basic approaches can and should be used with some degree of flexibility. Each report that you have to write will lend itself to one or other of the approaches suggested. You must select the approach which you think is most effective, and which allows you to present the information and ideas in the most meaningful way. This can, and very often does, depend on the content of the report.

6 Content

Collecting and organising the content of a report are vital steps in report writing. However well written a report is, it will fail if the basic facts and figures upon which it is founded are incorrect, inadequate or irrelevant.

Every comment, example, reference and suggestion included in a report must be well-researched, accurate, meaningful and relevant to the purpose of the report. Asking questions such as 'Does it add to the argument?', 'Is it new?', 'Does it make sense?' may help in eliminating some of the irrelevancies. The only way of making sure that the content is worth presenting is by painstaking, tedious and sometimes soul-destroying analysis, which leaves no doubt in the reader's mind that the report is based on a thorough study of the problem. Do not include points of which you are unsure or which you cannot substantiate if and when questioned.

Figure 6.1: Organising content

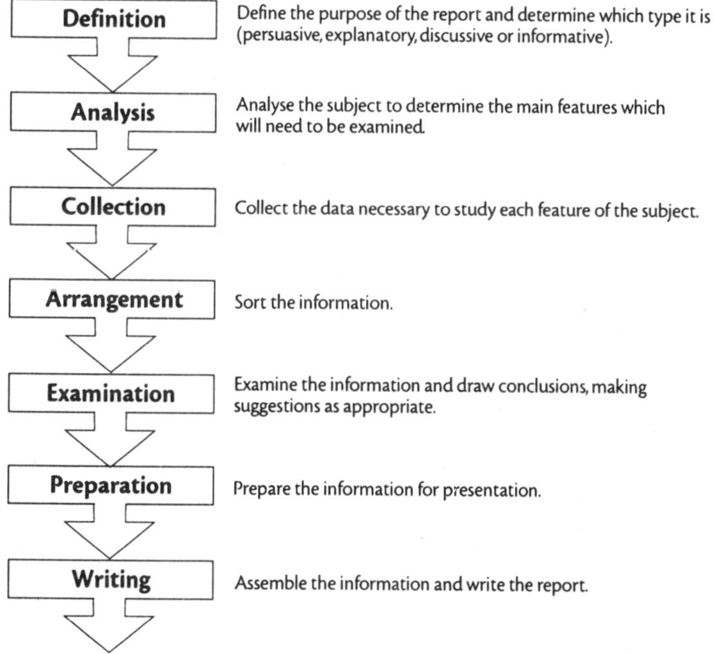

Organising content is a crucial job which should follow the steps listed in Figure 6.1.

6.1 Definition

You must always start by knowing why you are writing the report. Silly as it sounds, this is often the most difficult part of the whole process.

The dividing line between different types of report can be fine and only by knowing the purpose can the right approach be selected. This selection is crucial to the way in which the content of the report is produced. You may consider that the reasons are obvious; if you do, check. The obvious reasons are often the wrong ones.

6.2 Analysis

There are very few subjects which can be reported on without detailed analysis. Very often, people are so immersed in their own subject that they make assumptions which are far from true. They then call upon their specialist knowledge and experience in support of their opinions. There is never any harm in checking the validity of assumptions and studying the subject to separate the important aspects from the trivial.

Unfortunately reports are written, in which the greater part of the space is devoted to trivial items, giving scant attention to the really important ones. This can be avoided only by careful analysis of your subject.

6.3 Collection

The key activities that have to take place are:

- decide what information is required;
- discover the sources of the information;
- go to the sources and obtain the information;
- check that the information is accurate;
- check that the information is relevant to the subject.

These five simple sounding steps can, in fact, take even an experienced person quite some time to complete. The sources of information could be people, files, libraries, websites, previous reports stored in the computer system or in archives, or ones that simply do not exist. Access could be open, restricted or unavailable.

The source may be biased, hence the information must be checked, which is not always possible.

Ambiguity and contradiction must be eliminated by further questioning, until finally you are happy that the information is accurate, meaningful and relevant.

6.4 Arrangement

The information must now be sorted. This is the first point at which the layout of the report is considered. The easiest way is to make a file, which might quite simply be a manila folder, for each section of the report. The information is then sorted and placed in each of the files. When all the information has been found a home it is reviewed to see whether it is relevant to the section. When this sorting process is complete, consideration can be given to producing the report.

6.5 Preparation

The first stage in actually producing the report is the preparation of the material. Information in the form it has been collected (interview notes, extracts from books, sections of other reports) is rarely in the right form for presentation: it must be prepared. This may mean drawing graphs or diagrams, producing tables of figures, re-writing extracts, writing précis and re-wording verbal comments.

This stage can often take longer than actually writing the report. However, if this stage is ignored then it is certain that the resulting report will at best be longer than necessary, and at worst completely ineffective.

6.6 Writing

The actual process of writing the report will vary from person to person. You could dictate it to a person or machine, hand write it or type it directly into your computer or laptop. Choose the approach which feels the least constrained for you. You can also choose to write from beginning to end, from end to beginning, or in sections in any order.

Each of these approaches has its merits and the choice depends upon what comes easiest to you and the subject. The inexperienced report writer may find the 'beginning to end' approach the easiest to manage at first. If the previous stages have all been followed then the writing stage should not pose too much of a problem.

Write a first draft. At this stage only you need to be able to understand it. Leave it, if possible, for a day or two then revisit it to revise and edit. Correct it for logic and organisation; style and clarity; and spelling. This then becomes the second and, hopefully, final draft which is then converted into the final report. If it requires more work don't be afraid to reuse and redraft a number of times. Always number clearly the different drafts. This is particularly necessary if you are circulating them for comment prior to finalising the report.

Some people will always be better writers than others. However, if the stages of preparation as outlined above are followed, then even a moderate writer will produce a good report. Reports, thank goodness, stand or fall on the quality of the content, not on the literary style and finesse of the author.

7 Form

7.1 Report formats

The form a report takes will depend upon three factors:

1. the type of report;
2. the approach taken;
3. the content.

It is not necessary to decide on the form until the first draft is being prepared. It is only at this stage that the way in which the material is to be handled becomes clear. There are three classic formats that can be used:

1. **Logical** – Step-by-step presentation of each part.
2. **Sectional** – Dealing with each main feature in its entirety, section by section.
3. **Creative** – Where the writer deals with the subject in stages leading to a conclusion, but not necessarily in sequence.

7.2 Logical

The logical report is written in sequence, taking the reader from a specified starting point (introduction) to a definite end (conclusion) in a series of steps, each of which leads directly from the preceding one. Explanatory and informative reports are most frequently written in this style (see Example 2 on page 86).

The advantages of the logical report stem from the ability to take the reader step by step through the subject, so that by the time the conclusion is reached the report has achieved its aim. Unfortunately, such reports become rather tedious to read and, unless written in a brief, simple style, can be confusing in spite of being logical. The reason for confusion arising is in the handling of the content of the report, which can often require a good deal of back-tracking and cross-reference. When this occurs it tends to produce a disjointed format and the reader has to jump backwards and forwards.

7.3 Sectional

The sectional report overcomes the problem of the logical report by dealing with each feature of the subject in a separate section.

The sections are drawn into a meaningful whole by the introduction and the conclusion. The advantages for the reader are the opportunity to read each section without the need to refer to other sections and to draw conclusions in stages. The problem with the sectional report is the need to link sections. If attention is not paid to careful preparation it is possible to include irrelevant sections (see Examples 3 and 4 on pages 94 and 101).

7.4 Creative

This report is really a combination of the preceding forms. The basis of the creative report is the use of the content to convince the reader and most persuasive reports should be of this type. The creative report takes the form of a written discussion presenting ideas and comments in what appears on the surface to be an illogical sequence. However, when properly written, the creative report can be much more effective than one written in an apparently logical sequence (see Example 1 on page 81).

7.5 Guidelines on presentation

The following guidelines on presentation apply equally to the three classic report formats mentioned above:

- Use appendices to remove detail from the body of the report.
- Ensure the report can be read from introduction to conclusion without the need to refer to appendices.
- Provide a method of referencing to enable the reader to use the report.
- If the advantages are included make sure the disadvantages are also included. It is very often the case that when listed, the advantages outnumber the disadvantages.
- Use the minimum of words to make the point.

There is no one form of report that is better than another. Some organisations have established procedures for writing reports. Others leave it entirely to the individual. Unfortunately, you only know whether you have chosen the right form when you receive the reader's comments.

8 Numbering

The numbering of reports is a matter of choice and convenience. Numbering sections and paragraphs greatly helps in referencing both within the report and when referring to the report in other documents. However, numbering also fragments and subdivides in such a way that reading and clarity can be interrupted.

The way in which reports are numbered often causes people to adopt strong viewpoints from which it is almost impossible to move them. This is unfortunate because the purpose of numbering reports is to aid the reader and writer in the handling of the content.

8.1 Levels of numbering

There are three levels of numbering:

1. the report itself;
2. the sections of a report;
3. the content.

The way in which a report is numbered will depend to a large extent on the policy within the organisation. If there is a method of allocating a number to each report on a specific subject then it is a useful device. This would however require some form of central control. There is nothing to stop each department operating its own numbering system. Using self-explanatory titles and dates works quite well, but if the cost of administering a numbering system can be justified, it is preferable.

8.2 Sections

The content of reports should be clearly referenced so that the reader can pick out any part of the report. You can do this by numbering, sections, appendices and pages.

Sections should be summarised in the introduction and should each be allocated the first level of reference. This may be numerical or alphabetical. Whichever method is used for the main sections the appendices should be the opposite, i.e. if the main sections are numbered the appendices should be alphabetical and vice versa.

Pages should always be numbered sequentially starting with the first page after the title page. The page numbering can be straight through including appendices or separate for the appendices.

8.3 Content

The level of numbering within the content depends to a great extent on the detail and the way in which it is organised. It is possible to write a report consisting of main section headings and paragraphs, requiring only two stages of numbering. If, however, sub-paragraphs or lists are introduced then further stages of numbering need to be used.

8.4 Methods of numbering

The use of four forms of reference provides considerable scope in numbering reports:

- numbers – arabic and roman;
- letters – capital letters and lower case letters.

Any combination can be used so long as it aids the reader and is consistent. The numbering method used in the examples at the end of this book is as follows:

1 Section headings

1.1 Main paragraphs

1.1.1 Sub-paragraphs

(a) Lists within paragraphs

(i) Items within lists

A Appendices

This form of numbering is mainly decimal but changes at the fourth level to alphabetic and then to roman. The reason for mixing styles in this way is to avoid the references becoming awkward to use and to avoid confusion (see Example 3 on page 94).

Any combination of referencing styles can be used provided that it:

- is consistent throughout the report;
- covers every possible reference level;
- does not confuse the reader;
- helps the reader to use the report.

9 Production

The way the report is produced has an important effect on the reader's approach to it. The guidelines offered here are not exhaustive and professional printers and desktop publishing experts will be able to offer a variety of techniques which should meet the needs of most report writers.

Production can be looked at in several stages as described below:

- printed content;
- artwork;
- reproduction;
- binding;
- indexing.

9.1 Printed content

The vast majority of business reports will be printed. Even when they are presented and distributed on-line, recipients often print a copy for ease of reference. With modern computer systems and laser printers the results can be excellent, with a wide choice of options.

The typeface used will affect the appearance of the report and there are many different styles and sizes that can be employed to good effect. Computers allow an almost infinite choice. Proportional spacing of letters (i.e. the letter w taking up more space than the letter i) is almost invariable nowadays, though in some typefaces the spacing may be non-proportional (so that each character occupies an equal amount of horizontal space, regardless of its inherent width).

Choosing a typeface is important for appearance and readability. Lengthy technical reports tend to use serif typefaces such as Times Roman; management reports use sans serif typefaces such as Arial, though it is recognised that different people have different preferences.

Spacing of the content is very important. There should be adequate margins on the left and right, particularly on the left which is the most likely side for binding. Space must be left between sections and paragraphs so that they stand out. The level of content can be achieved by indenting. Too little on a page is far better than too much.

There are several conventions, all of which are intended to improve the readability and clarity of the content, and they also prevent typing errors. They also help with the appearance and presentation by providing consistency:

- if possible do not split paragraphs over pages;
- only use bold or underlining for headings and for recommendations/ conclusions;
- spell out numbers up to ten and then use figures above this (i.e. for 11 and above);
- never mix figures and words, e.g. 10 thousand;
- clearly number all charts and diagrams sequentially as Figure 1, etc.

9.2 Artwork

If any information is to be presented in a visual form, i.e. graphs, charts, photographs, then it should be produced according to the following rules (see also Example 4 on page 101):

- it must be directly relevant to the text and located as close to the point of reference as possible;
- it should be easy to follow and must make the point with impact;
- it must be referenced and titled;
- use a key where necessary;
- make sure the lines, bars, etc. are clearly identifiable;
- it must be well prepared by professionals if high quality is required.

If the above rules are followed then artwork can be extremely effective. Unfortunately, if the artwork is poor the effect is the exact opposite; it becomes a distraction and will spoil the report. Using 'clip art' can reduce impact if it is not used with sensitivity.

9.3 Reproduction

Today the vast majority of reports are reproduced on colour printers. The availability of high-speed, high-quality laser printers and photocopiers means that only reports needing to be copied in large numbers will have to be sent to professional printing services.

9.4 Binding

Binding has two values for a report. First, it improves the appearance and second, it protects the contents. There are a variety of binding systems available. Choosing which is the most appropriate will depend upon the following:

- the size of the report (thickness);
- the need for amendments to be made, i.e. fixed or loose leaf;
- the number of copies;
- the cost of binding methods;
- distribution requirements;
- the quality required;
- the need for special inserts, plans, maps, etc.

Binding should always be considered. There are several inexpensive systems available which can be used in any office to increase considerably the quality and appearance of reports.

9.5 Indexing

It is important that your reader can find their way around your report with ease. It will help, therefore, if you clearly indicate – with some form of dividers or index tabs – all the various sections and appendices.

Side indexing is normally done in two ways. The first is the use of an index card which is cut out to leave a small visible section. These are commonly used in ring binders for separating and indexing the contents. The other method is to attach a self-adhesive label which protrudes from the edge of the page and produces an effect similar to the card. These two methods are the most commonly used and are both very effective in helping the reader to use the report.

Care should be taken to see that the effort spent in preparing the report is not lost by lack of thought for the production requirements, which are often a decisive factor in the report's success.

10 PCs and Report Writing

For many people the PC (or personal computer) has replaced the pen. A great deal of writing takes place directly via the keyboard. This has advantages and disadvantages depending upon the expertise people have, and how fluidly they can use the machine while thinking about the content. Some people find it helpful, before approaching the keyboard, to draw up a plan of the report, together with notes on the content.

The PC will not of itself help you to produce good reports. Unless the basic rules of report writing are observed there is a danger of using facilities such as links to spreadsheets and graphics packages to make a complete mess of an otherwise good report. Of course these features can be used with good effect once the skill to produce simple readable reports has been developed.

There are a number of report writing software packages available but even if you are using a word processing package, PCs can help to produce attractive reports. This is provided that what they have to offer is used in an imaginative and creative way to enhance the simplicity, clarity, brevity and relevance of the reports you write.

Here are several ways in which PCs are useful:

- presenting information;
- organising and arranging information;
- writing and editing;
- proofing: spelling and word counts;
- grammar and style guides;
- publishing and layout software;
- WYSIWYG (see page 56);
- printing.

10.1 Presenting information

The medium you choose for presenting information will depend upon your circumstances and preference. However, whichever medium chosen the key factors of relevance, simplicity, clarity, conciseness, currency and accuracy still apply. No matter how sophisticated the possibilities these key factors should always be uppermost in your mind. Software and equipment provide an array of possibilities, from palettes of hundreds of colours to text in many different typefaces. Resist the temptation to dabble and hence turn a good report into a bewildering mess. There is a certain artistic skill in good layout and it is a skill in very short supply. Always remember: simplicity and clarity.

Whether information is presented on screen or paper it has to be read and must:

- be laid out with plenty of space;
- flow from left to right and top to bottom;
- use upper and lower case, except for headings;
- use no more than four colours including black and white.

Screen-based presentation offers considerable scope, especially if you have facilities such as Hypertext for accessing layers of information. If text-only versions of reports are to be placed on intranets or the Internet then these can be generated from MS Word, saving as HTML (Hyper Text Markup Language). If making up is done manually, remember that this will lead to two versions which will both need to be updated or revised to take account of any changes as time passes.

Windows also provides further facilities from a particular field on the screen. However, if not used with care these facilities can cause confusion. The basic principles of presenting information should always be followed regardless of the facility being used. Some people still prefer to read from paper and so they print off a copy. However, e-mail continues its popular growth and increasingly people are using the screen without the need for a printed version. There are additional considerations that need to be taken into account if you are moving to a screen-based version of your report. These range from formatting to security issues. It is enough for you to be aware of these differences so that you can seek expert help should you require it.

Visual presentation uses graphics and pictures in place of words. It is easy to provide both printed and screen-based pictures and graphs of very high quality. All the key factors of presentation should be considered, but the emphasis should be on simplicity, clarity and accuracy.

There is a very common and bad practice, which is to show the information using inaccurate scales. Making comparisons or showing movements in data should always show the full scale, i.e. starting at zero. If you are showing movements in interest rates, for example, and you start the scale at, say, 4% rather than zero, the extent of the change will seem much more significant than it really is.

Whenever you use graphics in a representative way, you should take care to avoid deceiving your audience. You should present the information accurately and with mathematical correctness. If necessary, add numbers to the graphs, particularly on pie diagrams.

Video and videotext are ways of presenting information on the screen, which with video, brings the possibility of movement and sound. The added power of the spoken word brings the pictures to life and adds a new dimension to presenting information.

10.2 Organising and arranging information

The PC offers a convenient and efficient way of organising materials. The basic idea of using folders that contain documents helps us to group material. This provides both a framework for managing the content, and a logical structure which helps you to move data, such as tables from a spreadsheet and charts from a graphics package, about and to reorganise it with ease. It also simplifies the control and backup procedures that you should follow to protect your work.

10.3 Writing and editing

The creation of the text should be a separate operation from editing. When creating it is important to allow a free flow of ideas, words and symbols from the mind onto the screen. You may find that you are tempted to edit as you go, but this is not the most effective way. Editing follows from reading what has been written, and not from writing. It is hard to switch from one to the other, and if you get them mixed up it leads to confusion.

When editing you might find it useful to do the following:

- remove unnecessary words from every sentence, i.e. restructure sentences to be simple and clear;
- remove unnecessary sentences from every paragraph;
- remove anything which does not add meaning and impact to what you are saying.

It is often easier to edit on paper than on screen, so make the amendments on paper before returning to the PC to edit your report. This not only gives you a break from the keyboard, but it also enables you to see what the text looks like on paper, and how clear it is to read and understand. When looking at the keyboard be a writer not a reader. When looking at the text on paper, read it properly as a reader might rather than as a writer.

10.4 Proofing: spelling and word counts

Re-read your document, preferably aloud, and note changes to spelling, use of words and grammar. Use the computer's spell checker (with great care, it does not always pick up all corrections). Ask someone else to read your report. A pair of fresh eyes can bring many useful insights.

Some software packages also offer a thesaurus which is an excellent way of ensuring that you avoid repeating the same word. It also helps you to find the shortest, commonest word to use.

A word count is useful because it helps to restrain verbosity and keep writing crisp. Some word-processing packages also compute a 'readability' index.

10.5 Grammar and style guides

Again use the PCs grammar checker with care. In some packages you can adapt them to incorporate your own preferences but there is no substitute for an opinion from an independent reader.

Grammar is intended as an aid to readability. It is a framework to help people write clearly and simply. Sometimes following the strict rules of grammar means that the writing is stilted, old fashioned and does not flow easily. Within reason, don't be afraid to bend the rules if it adds to clarity and readability.

To resolve doubts about grammar, refer to one of the many guides such as the *Complete Plain Words* by Sir Ernest Gower or *The Good English Guide* by Godfrey Howard (see the *Bibliography*).

10.6 Publishing and layout software

Once the report has been assembled it can be edited and blocks of text, diagrams etc. moved about to the best effect. Try not to deviate too far from your original intentions or you run the risk of losing the flow of your presentation.

The content of any report is your primary concern. No matter how you dress it up, rubbish is rubbish. Software does not help in any way with the preparation of the message to be conveyed by the report. We still have to be aware of all the rules of communication in determining what we want to achieve by constructing a message that we think the recipient will be able to understand and delivering the message in a language that the recipient will understand. Once we have completed this task we can use the system to prepare the document so that the desired message is emphasised.

The design and layout of reports involves a knowledge of typography, design, communication and graphic art. To assume that untrained people are going to be able to produce well-designed reports is nonsense. Unfortunately, if the design is bad it prevents the message from reaching the reader. The answer to this is either to employ a trained designer or to have such a person produce a set of layout standards for use on your system.

Report layout standards can answer such questions as:

- Where should the text go in relation to the graphics?
- Should the text be justified right?
- Should it be a one-column or a two-column block?
- Should we indent?
- Should we headline?
- How should we paragraph and sub-paragraph?
- How are we going to apportion space and decide upon borders, headings and footings?

This is no simple game where anything goes. If we get it wrong the results can be awful.

There is no denying that publishing and layout software is a very attractive and useful computer tool but like any tool it has to be used with the right degree of skill for the finished result to be what we want:

- First, ensure that the people you rely on to produce reports are fully trained as writers, designers and layout specialists.
- Second, make the software widely available for people to use in strict accordance with laid-down standards for design and layout. This should protect the finished product to some extent.
- Third, allow people to be creative and to experiment with what can be achieved with the software. This can of course lead to some horrible reports but it can also lead to some exciting and innovative ideas that would not have surfaced in any other way.

10.7 WYSIWYG

WYSIWYG (or What You See Is What You Get) is an acronym that describes a particular response from the PC to the user. It seems obvious to any user that the PC should display on the screen exactly what the finished product will look like when printed, and most now do. Unfortunately, not all software does this which leads to very odd looking reports.

When the document is printed the problems show up and require an additional editing process just to redo the layout. This should never be necessary and can be particularly troublesome in the case of tabular material (such as accounts), mathematical formulae, etc.

10.8 Printing

Pretty reports can hide the intended message beneath a surface of gloss. This may or may not be intentional but you only have to look at some of the annual reports produced by leading companies to see how easy it is to hide the truth beneath the smiling faces of directors and photographs of major assets.

The features of the laser printer should be used to emphasise the message and to reduce the content to the relevant few pieces of information that need to stand out from the rest of the less important facts.

11 Distribution and Follow Up

11.1 Distribution

Reports are normally produced with a particular audience in mind. This audience will become the distribution list.

It is important when sending the report to use a covering letter which explains why the person is receiving a copy and detailing the name of any other recipients. The actual distribution process must ensure that everyone receives their copy at the same time.

The covering letter should be headed with the title of the report and then briefly summarise its purpose. Any time scale for comment or dates of meetings should also be clearly indicated in bold type.

The order in which distribution lists are typed often gives rise to problems of status. It is much safer and easier to produce the list in alphabetical order than to try to follow the 'pecking order'. If there is one principal recipient then that name should be first; 'c.c.' to the others.

Confidentiality is another factor to be considered when distributing the reports. Many companies have established categories, which include or exclude certain personnel, but others have no such established approach. The safest approach is to ask the person responsible for requesting the report who should receive copies and how they need to be 'sent' to them.

11.2 Follow up

Having distributed the report it is important to follow it up by contacting each person on the distribution list once you think they have had a chance to read it. This contact might be very brief, just to check that people have received their copy and, if possible, to gauge their initial reaction. More detailed discussion may follow depending upon the nature of the report.

It is your responsibility to see that the report achieves its purpose and you must follow up to see that this happens.

One practical tip: circulate a reasonably finished draft of the report to one or two key people to obtain their views on the basis that the report can be altered to include their ideas before wider distribution. This has two beneficial effects:

1. First, the person concerned usually reads the report thoroughly and highlights errors and omissions.
2. Second, when the final report is circulated, these people are almost honour bound to support it, as they feel that it has already had their approval.

It may be necessary to write a follow-up report which shows how action stemming from the first report has been introduced and whether or not it is effective. Whenever a follow-up report is written it should carry the same title as the original report, possibly with a sub-title, and should refer to the original report in the introduction.

Part 3
Presenting Facts and Opinions

‘ Words like glass obscure when they do not aid vision. ’

Joseph Joubert,
Pensees

‘ Words are like leaves; and where they most abound
Much fruit of sense beneath is rarely found. ’

Alexander Pope,
An Essay on Criticism

This part provides further guidelines on presenting information in reports, on screen or as part of a spoken presentation. Of course information can consist of both facts and opinions, and it is vital that which is which is clear to the reader.

As much of business information is numerical or financial there is an emphasis in this part on presenting accounting information. However, the points being made can be applied equally to less numerically focused reports.

The ability to present information effectively is a primary requirement for anyone whose job it is to inform management. Unfortunately, it is not an activity that comes naturally or easily to the majority of people. This is particularly true of accounting information. It seems that people are locked into a straitjacket of columns and rows of figures.

Historically, accountants used ruled paper on which to write the numbers that were so important for measuring performance. Gradually, these manual documents were replaced by typed versions using special accounting typewriters that had extensive tabulation facilities so that the columns and rows could be maintained. Then came accounting machines that perpetuated the columns and rows presentation style. Finally, with the arrival of PCs (personal computers), the traditional approach was continued. So, even today, with the most sophisticated computers at our disposal, we are still producing accounting reports in columns and rows.

Accountants sometimes seem unable to think of any other possibilities. The very nature of bookkeeping requires that figures are kept in neat columns. To do otherwise would make it very difficult to carry out the essential arithmetic. The fact that PCs have changed the form of bookkeeping seems to have been lost on accountants.

But PCs have themselves helped to perpetuate the columns and rows concept. Spreadsheet packages have been designed both to cater for accounting needs and to foster the use of the computer's preference for using matrices. This preference is to make the mathematics easier to carry out, record and present.

It is worth asking the question: what do management want to see, our working notes or the results of our calculations? All too often, reports consist of working papers, with no explanations or with no clear identification of the issues. To compensate for this, managers are persuaded that they need to go on courses on finance for non-financial managers so that they can understand what accountants present to them. The role of accountants is often described as the interpretation of financial information – and no wonder. If we present management with our working papers, then of course we are going to have to interpret them!

12 The Importance of Relevance

When people want information they usually have a specific need. If, for example, managers want the current unit production cost of a particular product, they do not want a full production cost sheet with comparisons between actual and standard presented in columns and rows. They probably want to know something like this:

> Actual unit cost £18.21 which is £0.75 better than standard owing to a favourable price for raw materials.

This information is relevant for the particular need. If the need is not clear then a few questions should soon identify it. Asking managers what they are planning to use the information for is the first and most critical question. This can then be followed by more questions to ensure that the information provided is exactly right for the purpose for which it is to be used. This is the basic principle of relevance reporting.

Technology has helped us to rethink the ways that information, and particularly accounting information, can be stored, manipulated and presented to enable relevant reporting to replace old-fashioned and worn-out methods of presenting information.

12.1 Information: its value and purpose

Information is vital for effective management. Knowing what is happening, where and when, and identifying the effects on the business, are essential. This can only be achieved if the user's needs are understood, analysed and met in an efficient manner. There are many problems in effecting this. These problems are concerned with an understanding of the use and the value of information, as well as the skills of the people seeking to capture, distil and present it.

Our insatiable desire for information is driven by several needs.

12.1.1 Survival

Firstly, there is self-preservation against enemies. Knowing who our enemies are, where they are, their numbers and their weapons is basic to survival. Modern intelligence systems are based on discovering this information, albeit in a much more sophisticated way than that of our ancestors. Such information is only of value if it is available before the enemy attacks. It is useless to find out after the battle, even if it helps to justify why the battle was lost. So speed is of the essence, and hence the sophisticated systems that have been developed have almost all been concerned with speed in collecting and transmitting information.

In the commercial arena, corporate survival is equally dependent upon information about competitors, markets, new products, government policy and so on.

12.1.2 Risk

The second need for information is in measuring the degree of risk involved in a proposed course of action. There is always some element of risk; that the result of a proposed course of action will be different from that which is expected. It may be better or worse, but it will almost certainly be different.

If information increases knowledge and reduces risk then it follows that the more information is gained, the less is the risk. Just how far is this true? Is a point reached where more information is just unnecessary?

One way to decide what is enough is to examine each decision and assess:

- what we *must* know before we act;
- what we *ought* to know;
- what we would *like* to know.

We have to make many decisions without the benefit of this analysis. This may be due to timing or lack of understanding of the decision-making process, or simply a result of continuing the habits of a lifetime. In most organisations a balance is reached between the information that is available and the investment in information systems – but is this balance the right one?

12.1.3 Performance

Thirdly, we need information to tell us how well we are doing. Feedback is vitally important to successful decision making. Once we are in the middle of the battle we need information about the disposition of our troops, movements of the enemy, supply lines, ammunition, and a myriad detailed, logistical facts and figures. We have to have a constant flow of up-to-date information about what is going on and how well we are doing. This regular flow of information feeds the decision making about current operations and also influences the decisions we make about future activities.

The value of information is related to its usefulness at both strategic and tactical levels. So it follows that the first vital step for those responsible for corporate information is to establish exactly what the strategic and tactical needs are. For most organisations this will fall into three or four key activity areas which can then be built into an executive information system (see Chapter Thirteen). Establishing what these areas are, and concentrating investment and effort in them, can pay handsome dividends.

12.1.4 Presentation

Finally, good presentation of information is critical for its effective use. To have value, information must be useful. To be useful, information must be relevant, simple, clear, concise, current and accurate. These are the key factors but achieving them is not easy, and there are many pitfalls to avoid in the process. Perhaps the four worst pitfalls are:

1. too much;
2. too detailed;
3. too often;
4. too precise.

12.2 Relevance reporting

Information is relevant when it provides exactly what someone wants to know about a particular activity or event. Relevance is the provision of information about specified activities and events in accordance with the current needs of individual managers. This calls for considerable flexibility in the process of presenting information. It also implies that those responsible for presenting information will endeavour to relate information to the current needs of individual managers.

There are six essential steps in relevance reporting. These are:

1. establishing current information needs;
2. prioritising and targeting needs;
3. extracting relevant information;
4. choosing the presentation format;
5. assessing usefulness of reports;
6. adapting relevance reports.

All of these steps sound fairly obvious, yet they are all too frequently ignored.

The process used to collect, record, manipulate and store data has a value that is quite separate from the value of the information generated from it. Hence the primary value of corporate databases rests in the availability of the data, if and when it is needed. The primary value of information, however, rests in its relevance to specific decisions.

13 Numerical Presentation

A number is a symbol representing quantity. It is a symbol that can be used to manipulate data about quantities and, as such, is an extremely valuable concept. It is the basis of accounting and, to a large extent if not completely, the basis of computing. There is little doubt that to present numerical information in a textual form would be both time consuming and confusing. Presentation of information solely in a numerical form can, however, be difficult to read and may also lead to confusion. This topic of presentation is worth pursuing in greater depth as, however good the quality of information, it can be rendered worthless by poor presentation.

13.1 The need for a balanced approach

What is needed is a balanced approach. Unfortunately, the nature of computer-based information systems does not make this an easy prospect.

The widespread use of the columns and rows format for presenting numerical data has already been mentioned. This is perhaps the most common way of presenting numerical data but it is also the most difficult to read and use. A simple example of this is shown in Figure 13.1 overleaf.

The presentation itself is simple and clear, with only the significant numbers being shown. If, however, the report had been in £s instead of £000s it would have been almost unreadable. But, even in its present form, what is it intended to show, and how can the reader's attention be directed to relevant information? Even when the relevant information is spotted there is no explanation attached to it.

An alternative could be to present an extract of the relevant data supported by text explaining the implications.

Admittedly, for people who are used to reading columns and rows of numbers the alternative text style might not be an advantage, but for busy managers it can be a considerable improvement. If this information is presented on-line with the option for the manager to drill down to the detailed statement then we have the best of both worlds.

Figure 13.1: The columns and rows approach

PRODUCTION COST REPORT **JUNE** **All figures in £000s**

LAST MONTH				THIS MONTH			YEAR TO DATE		
ACT	BUD	VAR	MACHINE SHOP	ACT	BUD	VAR	ACT	BUD	VAR
272	240	(32)	Direct labour	231	220	(11)	1220	1150	(70)
350	360	10	Direct materials	311	300	(11)	1800	1900	100
40	36	(4)	Direct expenses	31	30	(1)	190	180	(10)
662	636	(26)	Total direct	573	550	(23)	3210	3230	20
23	20	(3)	Maintenance	21	20	(1)	130	120	(10)
7	6	(1)	Oils and greases	5	6	1	33	36	3
2	5	3	Cleaning	7	9	2	30	40	10
8	12	4	Internal transport	11	13	2	71	70	(1)
12	10	(2)	Cranes	13	10	(3)	72	60	(12)
6	8	2	Consumables	9	12	3	45	60	15
20	23	3	Supervision	21	23	2	130	138	8
4	5	1	Tool setting	11	5	(6)	52	30	(22)
5	6	1	Tool repairs	10	6	(4)	56	36	(20)
6	6	–	Lighting	6	6	–	36	36	–
21	20	(1)	Energy	24	20	(4)	140	120	(20)
16	14	(2)	Administration	15	14	(1)	90	84	(6)
130	135	5	Total indirect	153	144	(9)	885	830	(55)
792	771	(21)	Total machine shop	726	694	(32)	4095	4060	(35)

The presentation of numerical data can also be made pictorially rather than in columns and rows, and with current PC capabilities this can be effected easily. Graphical representation may still need to be accompanied by text, however, and this may be more difficult.

Perhaps the most powerful way to present numerical information is with a combination of numbers, text and pictures. This is perfectly possible with common software.

What is needed is essentially a combination of a spreadsheet, a graphics facility and a word processor. If a calculator together with a database facility for storage are also added then we have a powerful information presentation system. Such systems are readily available and are generally referred to as executive information systems (EISs).

When presenting numerical information, no matter how it is done, it is important to pay careful attention to three primary criteria, namely content, accuracy and significance.

13.2 Content

It is very easy to misunderstand the information needs that managers express, and thus to include information that is not required or to exclude that which is required, thus causing confusion.

Check carefully that managers understand the data that forms the basis of the information you present.

13.3 Accuracy

Most managers would say that the numerical data included in reports should be both complete and correct. But this should actually mean that it is sufficiently complete, and sufficiently correct, for the purpose for which the information is needed. With modern statistical facilities it is rarely necessary to have 100 per cent of the data to 100 per cent accuracy, even if this were possible. What is necessary is that we have enough data at the right time and to an acceptable degree of error. The amount of data we collect and the margin of error may well depend upon the speed with which we require the information.

In order to establish the desired accuracy we have to refer to the purpose for which the information is needed. We must also pay attention to the quality of the data being collected, especially when this data is entered into a PC and becomes part of an 'accurate' data processing system. There is a story about a sophisticated computer-based material control system that depended on a closing stock figure to calculate material usage. The stock figure was arrived at by banging the side of an enclosed silo with a large spanner and judging the volume of the contents by the resulting sound!

13.4 Significance

There is often a desire to present all the information even when a great deal of it is insignificant. When numerical data is presented in columns and rows the numbers should be limited to four or five digits across the columns. This may mean presenting the information in hundreds, thousands, tens of thousands, hundreds of thousands or millions. This makes the information easier to read and emphasises the key figures.

No matter how numerical information is presented, i.e. whether on paper or on the screen, the principles of good presentation still apply. PCs offer many advantages and allow considerable flexibility, but must be used intelligently, and with flair and imagination.

14 Presentation Styles

It is possible to distinguish five principal styles of information presentation which may be called illustrative:

1. military;
2. focus;
3. pin-point;
4. fishing;
5. haystack.

These styles offer a variety of options which should suit most people depending upon individual requirements.

14.1 The military style

This style is epitomised by the columns and rows approach discussed earlier. Everything is neat and tidy, and the numbers are in the exact position determined by their size and significance. The picture is one of order and discipline. Rank after rank of numbers march across the page, and readers find it hard to distinguish individual numbers from the massed ranks passing in front of their eyes. The order and neatness can give a false impression of the underlying content and value of the information. Who would dare to question such a well-formed and disciplined set of numbers?

14.2 The focus style

Here the emphasis is different. We may start with a block of numbers in a military formation, but then focus on individual numbers or blocks of numbers which have a particular relevance. This can be effected in several ways. For example, the focus can be introduced by text referring to the context from which the information has been extracted. Alternatively, the full military presentation can be shown and then the focus; or a picture shown with the focus expanding a part of it. The example in Figure 14.1 overleaf uses the second approach, where the full military style report is shown with the focus being indicated both diagrammatically and with explanatory text. Using modern hypertext systems enables this multi-level focusing to take place on the screen as the reader interacts with the information system.

Figure 14.1: Example of the focus style

PRODUCTION COST REPORT **JUNE** **All figures in £000s**

LAST MONTH				THIS MONTH			YEAR TO DATE		
ACT	BUD	VAR	MACHINE SHOP	ACT	BUD	VAR	ACT	BUD	VAR
272	240	(32)	Direct labour	231	220	(11)	1220	1150	(70)
350	360	10	Direct materials	311	300	(11)	1800	1900	100
40	36	(4)	Direct expenses	31	30	(1)	190	180	(10)
662	636	(26)	Total direct	573	550	(23)	3210	3230	20
23	20	(3)	Maintenance	21	20	(1)	130	120	(10)
7	6	(1)	Oils and greases	5	6	1	33	36	3
2	5	3	Cleaning	7	9	2	30	40	10
8	12	4	Internal transport	11	13	2	71	70	(1)
12	10	(2)	Cranes	13	10	(3)	72	60	(12)
6	8	2	Consumables	9	12	3	45	60	15
20	23	3	Supervision	21	23	2	130	138	8
4	5	1	Tool setting	11	5	(6)	52	30	(22)
5	6	1	Tool repairs	10	6	(4)	56	36	(20)
6	6	–	Lighting	6	6	–	36	36	–
21	20	(1)	Energy	24	20	(4)	140	120	(20)
16	14	(2)	Administration	15	14	(1)	90	84	(6)
130	135	5	Total indirect	153	144	(9)	885	830	(55)
792	771	(21)	Total machine shop	726	694	(32)	4095	4060	(35)

TOOL SETTING

Tool setting	11	5	(6)	52	30	(22)

The significant overspend on tool setting is due to four main reasons:

- the constant changes on the new computerised lathes;
- the learning curve for the fitters;
- the high failure of tools from our new supplier;
- the increased throughput.

TOOL REPAIRS

Tool repairs	10	6	(4)	56	36	(20)

The overspend on tool repairs is due to three factors:

- the high failure of tools from our new supplier;
- incorrect use of tools on the new computerised lathes;
- increased cost of materials, particuarly industrial diamonds and titanium.

14.3 The pin-point style

This is similar to the focus style except that the wider context is not considered. The information needed is pin-pointed by the manager involved and a report is prepared specifically dealing with the desired content.

14.4 The fishing style

This style is often used when people are unclear about what they want to know. It is rather like going out to collect data to see what turns up. It involves presenting information in such a way as to draw attention to things which seem interesting and then leaving it to the managers to spot the fish swimming in a sea of information.

The main technique for presenting information in a fishing style is to use a basic military style and then to highlight certain information. Ways of highlighting are:

- underlining, asterisks, boxes and circles on printed reports; and
- flashing, reverse video, underlining, colours and high intensity on screen-based reports.

This style may, in some cases, be adopted because information providers are nervous about actually focusing on or pin-pointing the information.

14.5 The haystack style

This is the style used by many accountants. It is based on the idea that the more information, the better. Every possible piece of information is given. Reports run to many pages of detailed information. There are summaries supported by ever-increasing levels of detail and different varieties of analysis. It is usually necessary to train new managers in the reading of reports, which come out with monotonous regularity and always in the same format. With these reports, managers are challenged to find 'the needle of pertinent fact in a haystack of irrelevance' – hardly a helpful approach.

Fortunately, the use of EISs and other database facilities, such as report writers, are helping to eliminate haystack reports.

All the styles mentioned above are evident in both printed and screen-based versions. The very nature of the use of screens can provide a much more selective approach to accessing and reporting information. So perhaps we will see much more use of the focus and pin-point styles of reporting in the future.

15 Presentation Pitfalls

There are many pitfalls in the effective presentation of information. These are mostly concerned with ignoring the key factors of relevance, simplicity, clarity, conciseness, currency and accuracy. Even when these factors are observed, however, it is still possible to trip over the matchstick of good intentions. Six of the principal pitfalls are described in this chapter and the names attached to them should aid recall.

15.1 The bear trap

Hidden deep in the forest of information, out of sight beneath a superficial cover of seemingly innocent data, lies a deep hole into which managers are likely to fall if they do not have their wits about them. Bear traps can be produced deliberately but most of the time they are created accidentally. They occur mainly when the level of information is too high for the purpose for which it is required. This may be through lack of time, laziness or the lack of a suitable level of data collection. Whatever the cause, the information is not provided at a sufficiently detailed level.

There is a bear trap in the information on machine shop costs in Figure 14.1 (see page 70). The information shows an underspend on direct materials. On the surface this seems fine, even though we know that throughput has increased. If we were to look a little closer we would discover that the underspend is due to the purchase of a supply of mild steel at considerably less than the usual price and below the normal specified quality. There was also some extra scrap and quite a lot of rework, which partly explains the overspend on direct labour. There is also the possibility of problems of product failure and the associated costs. Altogether this is quite a sizeable bear trap.

Bear traps are avoided by coming down to the forest floor and searching carefully through the undergrowth.

15.2 The creaky branch

If you can, imagine the organisation as a tree, with the trunk as the core of the business branching out into all the detailed activities. In this scenario, the information system is like the sap that feeds all these activities with the nourishment they need to stay alive and active.

Sometimes, if there is a problem with the way information is presented, it can cut the flow to a particular branch, which then begins to creak. It is not difficult for this to happen.

In our example company, we find a creaky branch – this is the stores activity serving the factory.

There is a stores system, and there is plenty of information about stock levels and issues and receipts. There is, however, very little information about the efficiency of the stores operation. Information such as the following is unavailable:

- cost per order;
- cost per requisition;
- cost of scrap;
- obsolete stock;
- stock outs;
- delays waiting for materials;
- wastage;
- price trends;
- range of goods in stock, leading to variety reduction;
- space utilisation.

True, this information may not have been asked for by the Stores Controller, but then this is part of the proactive service provided by information providers, or at least it should be. In the example, the stores function has become a very creaky branch indeed.

Creaky branches can be avoided by constantly looking at the organisation tree and examining how all the branches can be kept healthy by being fed with good, nourishing information.

15.3 The truth trap

Someone in the company said. 'The components had to be scrapped.' The truth of the matter was as follows. The Machine Operator said the tool settings were wrong. The Tool Setter said the program on the computerised lathe had a bug. The Lathe Manufacturer said the tools were set incorrectly. The Section Leader said it was because of the low-quality materials being used.

> *'There are many kinds of eyes, therefore there must be many kinds of truths, and consequently there can be no truth.'*
>
> ***Montaigne***

In presenting information there is no truth. There are facts and opinions. Presenters fall into the truth trap when they make statements which sound like truth but which are actually facts or opinions.

Truth traps can be avoided by remembering that facts are just that and opinions must be expressed as opinions. Comments such as 'I think', 'I believe' or 'in my opinion', should always precede opinions.

15.4 The quickie

Some managers request 'urgent' information about specific situations. This is perfectly reasonable. Information providers often react with a report that falls into the category of a 'quickie'. This is a report which pays more attention to the speed of presentation than the quality of the content.

Information must be relevant, current and accurate. The balance between currency and accuracy is such that the more accuracy that is wanted the longer it will take, and vice versa. Although 'fast' does not always mean 'inaccurate', there is a distinct possibility that if speed becomes critical then accuracy may be sacrificed.

The important element of providing speedy information and avoiding the quickie is always to express the likely degree of accuracy so that the user can use the information with a full understanding of its suitability for its purpose.

15.5 The pretty picture trap

There is a common belief that if something looks good it must be good. People also believe that if the price is high so is the quality. Both are self-evident nonsense but still people believe them to be true. Good-looking reports do not necessarily contain good-quality information. Managers have even been known to comment that the information must be correct as it came from the PC. Many people are seduced by pretty pictures and good-looking images.

There is no doubt that well-presented information can carry a higher degree of credibility than a scruffy-looking document – but is the content really better? Dressing up inadequate information does not make it adequate but it can make it seem to be. This is the pretty picture trap. By all means we should present information in the best way possible within reasonable cost limits, but we should not concentrate on appearance to the detriment of the quality of the information.

Examples of the pretty picture trap are common, particularly in corporate reports and information for employees. However, with modern PC facilities there is even more chance of falling into the trap when presenting routine management reports.

The pretty picture trap can be avoided by observing the following rules:

- Make sure that the improved quality of the presentation adds to the usefulness of the information. If it doesn't, then don't do it.
- Make sure that pictures, graphs, colours, etc. add impact and increase the usefulness of the information. If they don't, then don't use them.
- If the higher-quality presentation improves the simplicity and clarity of the information, without reducing currency and accuracy, then do it.

15.6 The full bucket

Consider the following:

> *'It is quite possible for management to collect more information than it can use to advantage, or which is more costly, or hinders production more, than the information is worth. This is a real danger that has to be guarded against continuously, for routine that serves a valuable purpose when initiated may cease to be useful by some later change of conditions.'*
>
> ***Elbourne***

This is the full bucket. It seems that we have to have every last drop of information. Even when the bucket is full we try to cram more in and in the process we lose some. Not only is the full bucket a heavy burden to carry but much information is lost through spillage. So what do we do? We get a bigger bucket!

One survey looked at the usefulness of 37 monthly reports from the information centre (computer department). The reports added up to some 2350 pages. The outcome of the survey was as follows:

- Seven reports were no longer used by anyone.
- Eleven reports were filed without being referred to.
- Fifteen reports were used to some extent, but improvements were suggested for all of them, usually for them to be simplified.
- Two reports were used extensively, but needed reorganising and summarising.
- Two reports were printed but not sent to anyone.

The result of the survey was that the overall number of reports was reduced to 18, most of which were shorter. Several of the new reports were exception reports focusing on specific customers, products, etc. The total number of pages was reduced from 2350 to 650. A procedure was also established for a continuous review of all reports.

16 Conclusion

Effective communication takes place when the transmitter constructs and delivers a message in such a way that the recipient gets and understands the message, and responds in exactly the way the transmitter intended.

This means that transmitters must know exactly what they are trying to achieve, and must select the best possible way of forming and delivering the message so that their objective is reached.

The golden rules for success are:

- simplicity;
- brevity;
- directness;
- impact.

When coupled with imagination, they will enable effective communication to take place. Complicated ideas, long words and sentences, and complex visual signals only get in the way.

This book has examined the principles of good communication. It has discussed communicating via the written word, the spoken word and visual signals. In all of these great emphasis has been placed on the importance of the way the message is received.

Simply because we can read, write, speak and hear does not mean we can necessarily communicate. Before we can do that, we have to learn how to transmit and receive messages. We have to practise what we have learned and we have to continually strive to improve.

Report writing is neither an art nor a science. If the guidelines set out in this book are followed it will be possible to write effective reports. No one is going to receive a literary award for report writing. The ability to write an effective report may, however, have a significant affect on your career.

A report will be effective if it is:

- short;
- readable;
- relevant;
- thorough; and
- useful.

Communication is about transferring ideas and information between people. It is the key to harmonious relationships, both socially and at work. Unless we gain the skill to communicate effectively, we will fail to be effective in many aspects of our lives. To be considered by one's peers to be a good communicator is perhaps one of the highest accolades we can receive.

It is interesting to note that good communicators stand out, because there are so few of them. The aim of this book is to help you become a good communicator. The rest is up to you to practise and improve.

Finally, please remember one thing – if people do not understand you, it is your fault, not theirs.

Examples

Example 1: a persuasive report

This report was written to recommend improvements in procedures for filing and retrieval of information by using microfilm equipment. Attitudes of the staff and managers involved were mixed, so a good case had to be made.

The report was accepted and implemented according to the recommendations in the report.

This example is based on a real report. Only the company, department names, dates and figures have been changed.

The report is an example of a persuasive report (see page 23) and is organised in the way suggested in this book. It was not necessary to produce appendices although it would have been possible to produce an appendix for section 5.2 on savings and benefits. On balance, however, it was felt more effective to leave this information in the body of the report.

The style of the report is creative (see page 42), always moving readers towards accepting the benefits until, by the time they read the section on costs, they are able to justify them.

Organisation and Method Report

Effective use of microfilm techniques and equipment

1. Introduction

1.1 The use of microfilm techniques is an extremely effective means of reducing clerical costs in the areas of filing and access to information. The principal values of using these techniques are:

1.1.1 Reduction in stationery costs

1.1.2 Speed of access to copy

1.1.3 Saving of space and handling

1.1.4 Improved file security.

2. Summary of recommendations

2.1 That the use of microfilming techniques be extended by the purchase of up-to-date equipment.

2.2 That the films so produced are used as basic reference files, rather than filing originals for immediate reference and films for long-term reference.

2.3 That the equipment be located in the user departments where it can be used on a regular, systematic basis.

3. Present position

3.1 At the present time there are two cameras and a reader-printer situated at Head Office. These are used as follows:

3.1.1 Purchase invoices for three divisions

3.1.2 Remittance advices for all divisions

3.1.3 Sales invoices for four divisions

3.1.4 Statements for four divisions

3.1.5 Conveyance notes for two divisions.

3.2 The films produced form a backup, filed centrally, to the copy files located in the departments concerned.

3.3 In order to provide the films for storage the following procedures are followed:

3.3.1 **Purchase invoices:** Originals filed in purchase department are removed from the file, filmed and then replaced on file. Files are retained for up to two years and the films are infrequently referenced.

3.3.2 **Remittance advices:** Top copy is de-collated, burst and dispatched to the supplier. The second copy is filmed in continuous form, then burst and filed.

3.3.3 **Sales invoices:** Top copy is de-collated, burst and dispatched to the customer. The second copy is filmed in continuous form, then filed.

3.3.4 **Statements:** Top copy is de-collated, burst and dispatched to the customer. The second copy is filmed in continuous form then burst and filed.

3.3.5 **Conveyance notes:** When the computer has finished with the tickets they are filmed batch by batch and then sent to the appropriate office.

3.4 The approximate number of documents filmed per annum is as follows:

Purchase invoices	150,000	takes 60 rolls film
Remittances	60,000	takes 25 rolls film
Sales invoices	350,000	takes 140 rolls film
Statements	180,000	takes 72 rolls film
Conveyance notes	600,000	takes 150 rolls films.

3.5 The methods of filing the documents are shown below:

Purchase invoices	Numerically within month within depots
Remittances	Alphabetically
Sales invoices	Numerically within division/region within month
Statements	Alphabetically within division/region
Conveyance notes	Numerically within day within depots.

4. Scope of survey

4.1 The present use of microfilm, and the continuing use of hard copy files, does not appear to offer any benefits, especially as referencing is done principally to the files rather than film. In addition, the use of files demands production of copies to fill them and the associated handling.

4.2 The equipment used at present was examined in the light of up-to-date equipment and the most effective means of using microfilm. The costs of existing stationery and films can be considerably reduced by concentration on one or the other, but not both.

5. Observations on recommendations

5.1 Systems approach to microfilming, depends on the use of the right equipment in the right place at the right time. This approach applied to the following documents can create significant savings.

5.1.1 Purchase invoices:
To be filmed in Purchase Department using existing camera, with facilities for reading, using existing reader/printer. One month's invoices on file, the rest filmed.

5.1.2 Remittance advices:
Filmed from continuous stationery, processed and filed in Purchase Department, where suppliers' queries are checked using existing reader/printer.

5.1.3 Sales invoices:
Filmed from continuous stationery, processed and sent to Area Sales Offices where customers' queries will be checked using new reader/printer.

5.1.4 Conveyance notes:
Filmed singly in Customer Queries section using new camera, and processed and filmed in Customer Queries section. Any queries from customers or depots will be answered by reference to film, using reader/printer.

5.1.5 Statements:
Filmed from continuous stationery and then dispatched to Customer Queries for processing, filing and reference.

5.2 Savings and benefits

5.2.1	Savings on computer stationery	£2,366	per annum
	Less additional cost of films and cassettes less processing savings	£ 331	
	Net annual savings	£2,035	

5.2.2 Other less tangible benefits:

less de-collating
less bursting
less filing
less need for storage space
less paperwork to handle speed of access to information ease of distribution.

5.3 Equipment costs and location

5.3.1 Equipment costs:

Continuous stationery camera	£2,250
Film processor	£2,350
Portable camera	£825
Reader printers (2 items)	£2,850
Reader	£179
	£8,454

5.3.2 The equipment will be located as follows:

Customer Queries	Processor	New
	Camera	New
	Reader/Printer	New
Purchasing Dept.	Reader/Printer	Existing
	Camera	Existing
Computer Dept.	Cont. stationery camera	New
Areas Sales Office	Reader/Printer	New
	Camera	Existing
	Reader	New

6. Conclusion

6.1 The recommendations in section 2 form the basis for a more efficient service to customers, suppliers and depots, and will considerably improve the existing methods of handling paperwork at Head Office.

Example 2: an explanatory report

Explanatory reports are not easy to write and so there are very few good examples available. The report contained in this example is based on one written some years ago. The names have been changed and the circumstances altered so that the project is no longer recognisable.

This example of an explanatory report covers all the main points discussed earlier (see page 23). The appendices mentioned in the example have been excluded because of space; they would have added little to the value of the example. Most of the appendices were attached as evidence where it was felt necessary to do this to support comments within the report.

The report has been prepared in a logical style (see page 41), taking the reader step by step through the content, adding additional facts as each paragraph is read. Numbering is important as on several occasions it is necessary to cross-refer to an earlier paragraph.

Following the receipt and discussion of the original report the company concerned re-appraised its cost control procedures and made a number of changes.

Collington Terminal

A report on the reasons for the loss incurred on the contract

1. Introduction

1.1 This report has been prepared to explain the circumstances which led to the completion of the Collington Terminal contract at a loss of £250,000. The report has been prepared by an investigating team headed by Trevor Bentley, a senior executive with the company and a Chartered Management Accountant.

1.2 The report is intended to provide a complete picture of the events leading up to, during and upon completion of the contract. To do this effectively the team were given authority to interview any persons they wished and to examine any documents they considered relevant to the subject under scrutiny. This report is the outcome of the team's investigations.

2. Persons involved

2.1 In order to avoid confusion, all persons and departments involved will be referred to by titles. In certain cases the title has been abbreviated, as shown below in brackets:

Contract Manager
Chief Estimator
Area Accountant
Central Buyer
Client
Architect
Structural Steel and Foundation Contractors (SSC)
Plant Manager
Site Foreman
Site Planning and Control Engineer (SPCE)
Construction Director

3. Sequence of events

3.1 The company was first approached by the client in January 1985. At this time, the idea for a Collington Terminal was a vague one. The client had not fully considered the problems concerned. The client commissioned the company to examine the feasibility of such a terminal and to produce initial plans suitable for submission for outline planning permission.

3.2 The sequence of events from this report to the client accepting the company tender were as follows:

Date	**Event**
12 Jan 1985	Company employed an architect to produce a basic proposal.
23 Feb 1985	Company received the basic proposal.
3 Mar 1985	Proposal was discussed at board meeting.
6 Mar 1985	Amendments submitted to architect.
18 April 1985	Architect submitted draft plans.
4 May 1985	Company accepted draft plans.
2 June 1985	Company produced a project proposal (Appendix A) for the client.
16 July 1985	Clients accepted the proposal subject to a number of amendments and requested that the company submit a tender (Appendix B).
24 Oct 1985	Company submitted a complete tender.
19 Nov 1985	Client accepted the tender and signed the contract.

3.3 During the above sequence of events, full and detailed investigations were carried out on the site by the company's normal contractors for structural and foundation work. The report from SSC indicated a need for deep foundations requiring pile driving. This had been allowed for in the contract price.

3.4 On 25 November 1986 the company appointed a contract manager and a meeting was held to discuss the contract. This was attended by:

Contract Manager

Architect

Chief Estimator

Area Accountant

Site Planning and Control Engineer (SPCE).

3.5 The meeting agreed the approach that should be taken to the contract and asked the SPCE to produce detailed plans and schedules of material requirements. The minutes of the meeting are attached as Appendix C.

3.6 On 4 January 1986 a second meeting was held comprising the same people with the addition of SSC. At this meeting the contract schedule (Appendix D) was approved.

3.7 On the day following the meeting the client was sent a copy of the schedule with a proposal that work should commence on 1 April 1986.

3.8 The contract started on the due date and continued without any problems until 29 August 1986 when the monthly progress report was produced (Appendix E). This showed that expenditure on structural steel, concrete and plant hire, all concerned with foundations, was higher than the original plan.

3.9 The contract manager called a meeting on 4 September 1986 attended by:

Area Accountant

SSC

Architect

Chief Estimator

Central Buyer

SPCE.

3.10 The meeting resolved that due to geological problems the contract would need to be extended by two months and that the client should be approached with a view to obtaining an increased price.

3.11 The contract manager and architect approached the client on 10 September 1986. The extension to the contract was agreed but no further price increase was accepted.

3.12 The project continued until 3 December 1986 when the site foreman reported a crack in one of the main pillars. The fault was investigated the same day and the contract manager authorised a reinforcement of the foundations.

3.13 The contract proceeded without further problem until the following April when a progress report was received by the construction director. This showed a significant increase in the cost of structural steel supplies.

3.14 On 28 April 1987 the construction director held a meeting with the contract manager and SSC. At this meeting the causes for the increased costs were discussed and the construction director sanctioned the final supplies required to complete the contract.

3.15 On 4 May 1987 the contract manager was formally reprimanded by the construction director and moved on to a different contract. On the same day the construction director wrote to SSC indicating that on completion of the contract SSC would not be working for the company again.

3.16 The contract was completed on 23 June 1987.

3.17 The final contract accounts produced on 11 August 1987 indicated a loss of £250,000.

3.18 At the board meeting on 5 September 1987 it was decided to carry out an investigation into the Collington Terminal contract.

3.19 On 12 October 1987 this report was presented to the construction director.

4. Action taken

4.1 There were several key actions which contributed to the loss on the Collington Terminal. These were (the reference in brackets is the paragraph number of the sequence of events section):

- 4.1.1 Preparation of project proposal (3.2)
- 4.1.2 Structural Steel and Foundation Contractors' report (3.3)
- 4.1.3 Submission of the tender (3.2)
- 4.1.4 Preparation of the control plan and materials schedule (3.5)
- 4.1.6 Meeting on 4 September 1986 (3.9)
- 4.1.7 Site foreman's report on 3 December 1986 (3.12)
- 4.1.8 April 1987 progress report (3.13)
- 4.1.9 Meeting on 28 April 1987 (3.14)

4.2 Each of these key factors is analysed below. No conclusions have been drawn by the investigating team. Where the words are those spoken by the person concerned they appear in square brackets, i.e. [ ], otherwise the following comments are reported on the basis of the team's interpretation.

4.3 Project proposal (Appendix A)

This was prepared by the contract manager, the architect and SSC. It was a broad proposal which gave an indication of the project time-scale, an outline of the structural approach, an artist's impression of the finished job and a statement of main constraints.

One of the constraints mentioned was the need for special foundations if the terminal was to be built on the client's site.

4.4 Report of SSC

The team has been unable to trace any form of written report other than a letter from SSC stating that it would need to have some special pile driving equipment for the contract. Any other information had been given verbally. The chief engineer at SSC had stated quite categorically that he discussed the difficulties of the foundations with the chief estimator and the architect at the time when the tender was being prepared. Though both of these men recall the meeting neither of them remembers the specific details and are in one accord that the SSC engineer had stated that [the job would be a piece of cake].

4.5 Preparation of the tender (Appendix B)

The tender was prepared by the chief estimator. He was given full details of the structural steel concrete and plant hire from SSC who only quoted for labour. The company was therefore responsible for obtaining prices on these items. The chief estimator stated that due to the pressure to complete the tender he had used the latest prices for steel and concrete given to him by the central buyer and then he [added a contingency allowance of 10% for inflation and quality variations]. The plant hire had been arrived at by [inspired guesswork] as it was unusual plant that the company had never used before. These three major items, together with site clearance and preparation, made up 52% of the contract cost.

4.6 Contract plan and material schedule (Appendix D)

The detailed plan and material schedule was prepared and used as a basis for forward ordering of materials. By reference to the orders it was clear that the price of steel at the time of ordering was 15% higher than that used in the tender This was either not checked or was overlooked as no one we interviewed had noticed the fact. The planning and control engineer had recognised a discrepancy in the quantities which he pointed out to the contract manager. When they checked, it appeared that the figures given by SSC were 20% short of those required. To ensure the quantities agreed with the schedule the contract manager reduced the pile depth by 20%.

4.7 August progress report (Appendix E)

The progress report was prepared by the area accountant and showed that more had been spent on structural steel and concrete than was allowed for in the whole contract and 80% of the plant hire allowance had been spent. The work done statement indicated that the main site work was only 70% complete and that a further £80,000 would be needed for further supplies of steel and concrete to complete. The area accountant had discussed the report with the contract manager and SPCE.

4.8 Meeting on 4 September 1986

Contrary to general procedure no minutes were kept of this meeting. All those who attended were interviewed and it appears that the main discussion centred on the problems with the foundations. An argument developed between the contract manager and the SSC engineer. This covered the reduction of piling depths which occurred when the material schedules were being examined (see 4.6).

Each man blamed the other for the fault. It was decided to put the problem right and seek further money from the client. The client refused to pay any more.

4.9 Site foreman's report

On 3 December 1986 the site foreman reported (verbally) a crack in a main pillar. The contract manager examined the crack with the SSC engineer who blamed the contract manager with the comment [if you hadn't reduced the pile depths this would not have happened]. The contract manager authorised the strengthening of the foundations which required more materials.

4.10 April 1987 progress report

The progress report produced in April 1987 showed a further increase in material costs. This had not shown up earlier because the invoices had been delayed somewhere in the paperwork chain. Nobody would admit to sitting on the documents. The construction director arranged a meeting for the 28 April 1987 prior to which he had a detailed discussion with the contract manager. In this discussion, the construction director made it quite clear that he held the contract manager responsible for the loss. Subsequent to the meeting the contract manager was formally reprimanded and downgraded to the Small Works Department.

5. Cause and effect

5.1 From the information gathered it would seem that there were three principal causes for the loss on Collington terminal. These were:

1. The price quoted to the client was not adequate to cover all the costs of structural steel, concrete and plant hire.
2. The lack of a formal report on the foundation requirements led to the analysis of material requirements being far lower than required.
3. The change of pile depths in order to reduce the materials caused the crack in the pillar and the extra cost of strengthening.

These three prime causes led to the over-expenditure on the materials concerned although a subsequent measure carried out by the investigating team indicated a discrepancy in materials used and records of receipts on the site to a value of £40,000. No satisfactory answer has been obtained as to the cause of this discrepancy.

6 Conclusion

6.1 This report highlights the importance of the full examination of site conditions before tendering as well as the need for careful evaluation of tender prices. The disciplinary action of the construction director may have been desirable but flaws in the overall supervision of the contract allowed major over-expenditure to occur until it was far too late to correct the problems.

It is suggested that the company reviews its contract cost control procedures at the earliest opportunity.

Example 3: a discussive report

This example provides an example of a discussive report in the form of a systems proposal. The particular example given is based on an actual report and only the company name has been changed.

The report sets out the main points for discussion in the form outlined earlier (see page 24). The content of the report is quite specific but leaves room for discussion. No section includes suggestions which could not be amended in the light of the discussion.

The report follows the sectional approach (see page 42) although it could be claimed that there is a certain logic in the way it is set out.

It is also a good example of methods of numbering (see page 44) showing how different levels of numbering can be used.

The report was fully discussed at a meeting following which an action plan was agreed and subsequently implemented. The chair at the meeting issued an agenda comprising each of the main section headings. This ensured that the report was fully discussed, and added order and control to the meeting.

Systems Proposal

Systems proposal for reward contractors

1. Introduction

1.1 This report has been prepared as a basis for discussion on the development of systems in Reward Contractors. In addition to dealing with the specific requirements of Reward Contractors the principles of systems development within the group as a whole will be outlined.

1.2 The preparation of this report is the result of visits made by systems personnel to all areas of Reward Contractors in addition to two recent visits to the North East and Scotland when the principles embodied in the suggestions were discussed with the local managers.

2. Scope of systems requirements

2.1 Reward Contractors' existing systems revolve around the accounting control procedures operated at the Regional Offices and at the Head Office. The accounting systems have been designed to ensure accurate financial control and to provide information to management. The systems do provide accurate financial control and do provide a degree of management information. In respect of management information, however, the needs of local management, particularly regarding operating control, are not fully catered for. This is highlighted by the different operating systems and the extraction from local records of other information thought to be of value.

2.2 It is suggested that the existing systems are:

(a) too slow;

(b) lacking in operational control data;

(c) too financially oriented.

It is not implied that the existing financial control should be reduced but that the detailed level of control be examined to reduce clerical effort and improve the value of the information produced by the system.

2.3 In short, it is suggested that the system should be based on providing management information with financial controls rather than financial control systems with management information.

2.4 The implications of these suggestions for the future systems development is threefold:

(a) a change of emphasis on the basis of the system framework;

(b) a change of methods to utilise modern facilities;

(c) a development towards computerisation to speed up data flow and reduce peak working.

3. Suggested approach

3.1 Systems development in the group is based on the following principles:

(a) All systems must be designed by management with specialist help and advice.

(b) Systems must be designed to provide maximum flexibility at the user end, whilst using standard computer-based methods and controls.

(c) Where computer facilities are required these can be obtained in two ways:

(i) using the group computer centre;

(ii) using outside computer resources.

(d) Systems projects should be approved by the management concerned and the benefits being sought should be clearly stated in financial terms.

3.3 The operating systems should be the basis of the control systems and should provide a data flow, from which detailed data is used locally for operational control. It is then summarised and cross-checked within the system to provide financial control information leading to the production of final accounts.

3.4 There are instances where the benefit of being in the group and using similar systems can be clearly seen. One particular interaction is on the buying of materials. It is possible for the supplying Division to provide the following information from the central computer files:

(a) Up-to-date prices for every material currently being delivered to every Reward Contractors' site, separated by cost centre and contract. This would enable the accurate preparation of invoices without delay and allow accurate material costs to be posted to the contract cost records.

(b) Detailed schedule of materials purchased by Reward Contractors, replacing Supplies Division invoices and avoiding, to a large extent, detailed checking of invoices. (A single invoice could be raised for each region to cater for VAT.)

3.5 Since these points were raised with managers in the North East and Scotland steps have been taken to ensure these facilities can be made available if required. This could be done in a matter of two or three months.

3.6 In order to ensure that management is fully involved with the project it is suggested that a Project Team is formed comprising the following:

(a) Group Systems Project Controller;
(b) Systems Accountant;
(c) an Estimator;
(d) a Contract Manager;
(e) a Regional Manager.

3.7 The Project Team should be chaired by the Regional Manager and would be a working team. Each member would be given specific tasks to perform and would therefore need to give up some time, particularly in the initial design stage. When the agreed system requirements are handed over to the Systems Development Section at HQ for analysis and programming the Systems Accountant could act as the co-ordinator. In addition, he should also act as secretary to the team. This method of operation has been found to work very well.

3.8 It will be necessary for the Project Team to investigate the following areas of activity in detail, and to collect data relevant to the subsequent design of systems:

(a) estimating;
(b) contract set up and scheduling;
(c) contract administration and reporting;
(d) contract costing and control;
(e) measuring and invoicing;
(f) sales ledger and credit control;
(g) purchase ledger;
(h) accounting procedures and controls;
(i) management reporting requirements.

3.9 Other activities, namely manufacturing, will be included and recommendations made on how these activities can be linked into the main systems.

4. Contract control system

4.1 It is believed that regular information (weekly) for contract monitoring and control is fundamental to improved profits. Though other systems, namely sales ledger, have benefits, it is considered vital that development is based on a contract control system.

4.2 The proposed system includes a weekly contract report which would show the actual costs for the week and the accumulated costs for the life of the contract. It would compare these with the estimated cost of the work done to date. This would be the Contract Manager's main control report.

4.3 The above is only an outline, but it can be seen that the ability of the system to calculate and compare progress in this way is an important step forward in providing management information.

4.4 Cost increase formulae could be incorporated, as could latest material prices, but these sophistications would need to be examined in detail to determine their value.

4.5 The control information would be used in the accounting procedures and the goods received report would provide a basis for checking invoices.

4.6 The system would be used by local management to monitor progress and to determine at an early stage that actual events are deviating from the plan allowed for in the estimate. The information of measures and up-to-date prices should enable more rapid invoicing although it is appreciated that there is no substitute for the on-site measure.

4.7 **The advantages of the system are:**

(a) rapid information;

(b) comparison with estimate for corrective action;

(c) it is based on current practice;

(d) reduced effort;

(e) virtual elimination of peak working conditions in regional offices;

(f) potential cost benefits are considerable, e.g. an increase of 1% in actual gross margin is equivalent to £140,000. (The difference between estimated gross margin and actual gross margin is

running at between 4% and 8%.)

4.8 Disadvantages:

(a) Improvement in daily reporting techniques could mean some extra work for foremen and supervisors.

(b) Additional work for estimating in providing the contract file data

(c) The change of approach which will require new documentation, new equipment and new styles of reports.

4.9 The contract monitoring and control system, being the hub of the system wheel, will need to be linked to the following systems:

(a) sales ledger;

(b) purchase ledger;

(c) payroll;

(d) plant;

(e) accounts (nominal ledger).

These systems may or may not be using compatible software and so it will be necessary to provide the flexibility to cope with system integration.

5. Resources

5.1 It is not felt that additional staff will be required in Regional Offices. It is too early to make specific forecasts.

5.2 A systems development team of one analyst and two programmers will be required for the equivalent of one person year. This can be one of the existing teams or a new team depending upon the priority and the timing.

5.3 It is believed that a network of computers capable of:

(a) data input;

(b) data transmission;

(c) data output; and

(d) data storage;

will be required in each Regional Office and at Head Office.

5.4 It is also considered necessary for these to be able to communicate with the computer centre to either:

(a) the existing computer, possibly extended to cater for the additional systems; or

(b) a new computer server dedicated solely to this task.

5.5 The anticipated cost of the above requirements is:

(a) systems development team – three men for one year £95,000;

(b) terminals at each of Regional Offices and Head Office (six total) at £2000 = £12,000;

(c) central and network facilities £20,000;

(d) annual maintenance costs for equipment £2000.

These costs are only estimated, but are within ±5%.

6. Courses of action

6.1 The stages in providing the benefits outlined are:

(a) approval of this report;

(b) formation of the Project Team;

(c) initial plan of resources;

(d) formulate the overall programme;

(e) detailed investigation;

(f) preparation of systems requirements;

(g) selection of equipment;

(h) ordering of equipment;

(i) detailed analysis and programming;

(j) testing;

(k) training;

(l) implementation;

(m) review and evaluation.

At each of these stages, approval will be sought from the Reward Contractors' Board before proceeding. A final evaluation will be done to show the degree of success achieved and is normally prepared one year after implementation.

7. Conclusion

7.1 This report is aimed at obtaining approval to the further investigation into the form of the systems required by Reward Contractors. It is not intended to specify precisely what the system should be, but rather the direction in which we should go to improve the information available to management and thereby increase the overall profitability of the company.

Example 4: an informative report

This example of an informative report is an actual report in which only the names of companies and locations have been altered.

In this report are examples of several features of report writing. These are:

- the basic approach to writing an informative report (see page 24)
- the sectional style of report writing (see page 42).

You will notice that the report provided an opportunity to make further recommendations (section 2) and also to express thanks to the people concerned (paragraph 8.3).

There is also a persuasive element in this report, but the primary aim is for the report to inform people of what has happened.

Vehicle Utilisation

Pilot scheme evaluation report

1. Introduction

1.1 The scheme has now been in operation for two full months (May and June). From the introduction of Loadplan in April, records have been kept of the performance of the company vehicles in the scheme and those company vehicles outside the scheme. This report indicates the results of the analysis of this information and recommends further action.

2. Recommendations

2.1 That Loadplan continues to be operated in the pilot scheme area as an operational system (see sections 4 and 5).

2.2 That Loadplan be introduced into a further group of quarries in the Northern area (see section 6).

2.3 That consideration be given to the way distribution is organised in the Eastern Area to optimise on the Loadplan system.

3. Analysis of results

3.1 Earnings per vehicle day have increased throughout the period of operation of Loadplan. This increase is shown in the following charts (see Figure 1 and Figure 2).

3.2 The average earnings of the company vehicles in the pilot scheme and those outside are shown in Figure 1.

3.3 The earnings of individual vehicles have been recorded and compared to the average earnings of the whole of the company fleet. Figure 2 shows that over the period of the scheme more and more of the vehicles subject to Loadplan have exceeded the fleet average.

3.4 During the pilot scheme, circumstances have varied from depot to depot, as has the understanding and acceptance of the Loadplan system. These points are discussed fully in section 4 of this report. It is almost certain that the solution of some of these difficulties will lead to further improvements in the performance of vehicles.

Figure 1: Comparison between pilot scheme and rest of the fleet

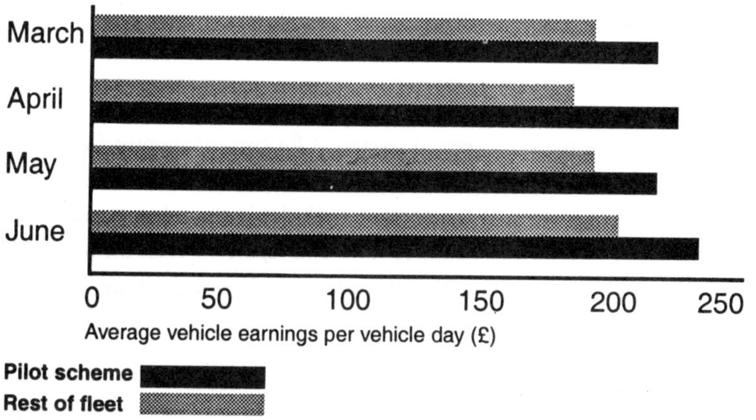

Figure 2: Record of pilot scheme vehicles

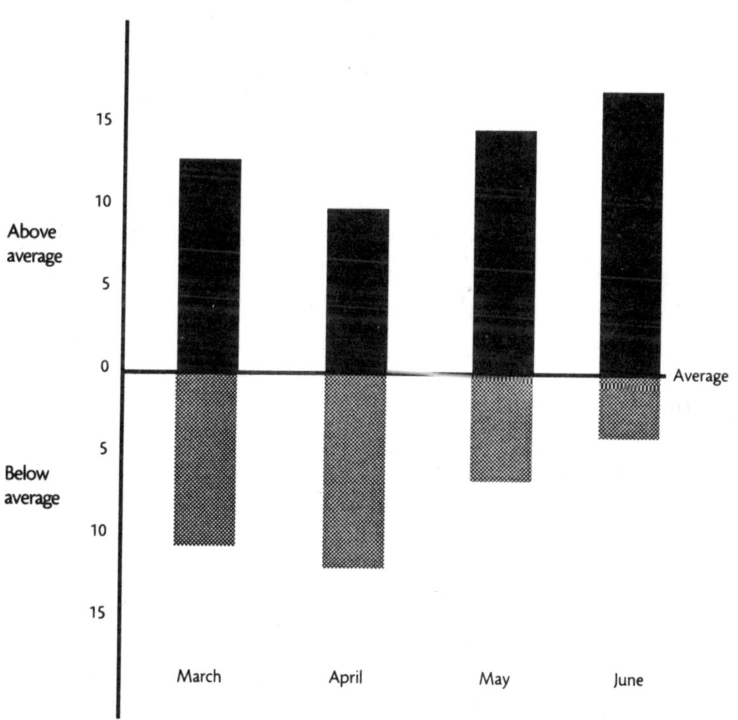

4. Operational environment

4.1 In any pilot scheme the full importance, advantages and disadvantages of the basic system only appear under realistic working conditions. Being new, the scheme is the subject of scrutiny and comment from both informed and misinformed personnel who may or may not be directly involved with the day-to-day working of the system. Loadplan is no exception and has undergone trials in a working environment since April using 23 vehicles at the following units: Cockby, Sugar Wharf, Friarton and Morton.

Loadplan has been introduced by O & M with the assistance of a full-time Loadplanner regularly visiting each site and co-ordinating vehicle utilisation daily. Fax machines have been introduced at each unit and at the control centre at Wellington. Set out below are the salient features of the successful Loadplan implementation at these sites.

4.2 *Cockby*

Owing to the absence of a permanent full-time weighbridge clerk the scheme has not had a good start.

It would appear that during the trial period orders were satisfied direct from production rather than stock. Production was interrupted on a number of occasions due to plant breakdowns. This caused a reduction in work available for vehicles, which was not always reported to the Loadplanner in time for re-allocation of vehicles to alternative work. The problems were, however, recognised by the Loadplanner during the latter part of the trial period and vehicles were re-allocated. Loadplan highlighted the non-utilisation of vehicles at this site and the actions of the Loadplanner ensured that alternative work was found. Whilst it may be argued that such action might have been taken in the absence of Loadplan, it is considered unlikely.

4.3 *Sugar Wharf*

During part of the trial period the weighbridge operator was absent due to sickness. This meant that Loadplan training and implementation was not done under the most favourable conditions. Loadplan sheets have had to be completed in retrospect, often by the Loadplanner himself. The fax machine is considered to be a great advantage by weighbridge and production staff in both the dry and coated materials plants. Errors in order information have been eliminated, as has the laborious task of taking down information by telephone at inconvenient times.

The dry materials plant manager considers that Loadplan has given him greater access to company vehicles because starting and finishing times have improved. He is also of the opinion that the full advantages of Loadplan would be seen if all loads, including hired hauliers, were planned. This is a natural development of the system which would avoid too many vehicles chasing too few loads. This would ease traffic congestion and ensure that the hauliers who remain obtain a full day's work.

4.4 *Friarton*

The system has been fully accepted by an experienced and knowledgeable weighbridge clerk who organises and monitors his own Loadplan within the system. The fax machine has been of considerable assistance in ensuring that orders are passed in time for vehicles to be loaded for the following day's first drop and buffer work is available for opportunity loads. In addition, there is excellent co-operation between this site and Morton to maximise vehicle utilisation at both locations in the light of changing short-term and unexpected workload requirements.

4.5 *Morton*

Again the system has been fully accepted by an experienced weighbridge clerk who is regularly operating the Loadplan system with nine company vehicles, most of which are generating high average daily earnings.

The high daily tonnage at this unit and the operation of a large number of company vehicles has maximised the use of the fax machine which is now considered by the weighbridge clerk to be vital to his overall efficiency.

The excellent vehicle utilisation at this unit also reflects, to some extent, the pre-loading of vehicles for the next day and the availability of buffer work for opportunity loads within the Loadplan framework.

4.6 The Loadplan system has thus been tested under actual working conditions and has stood the test well. In addition, it has caused local management, weighbridge, traffic and distribution staff to examine their actions and to consider the consequences of such actions on the utilisation of transport to the benefit and well-being of the company.

5. Changes and improvements

5.1 A pilot scheme by its very nature tests a basic system under working conditions and results in the proving or otherwise of that system. At the same time, areas for improvement arise. The figures presented earlier in this report have, we believe, proved the success of Loadplan. It is felt that the following changes in the system's operation will improve its efficiency.

5.2 The daily order sheet is being re-designed in order to improve the use of fax machines.

(a) Provide for the passing of up to 17 (previously ten) orders during one transmission period of six minutes.

(b) Minimise the transmission time required when less than a full sheet of orders is available for transmission, thus making the transmission of even one order cost-effective.

(c) Enable the Loadplan to be transmitted with the order sheet thus avoiding the need for another transmission or telephone call.

(d) To facilitate the sending of dry and coated orders on one sheet whilst still keeping the types separate for dispatch to different addresses at the receiving site.

5.3 Examination of related systems has highlighted the need for a redesigned delivery ticket (on which information is passed to the Area Sales Office) to assist the weighbridge clerk in his clerical activities.

(a) There is a requirement for a 'cumulative tonnes' column to enable the weighbridge clerk to check the tonnage delivered at any time without keeping a separate record.

(b) The present requirement for separate delivery tickets for each type of material being delivered to the same customer is wasteful of clerical effort at the weighbridge.

These problems cannot be overcome immediately owing to effects on the computer system. However a study is being made with a view to developing a simpler method.

5.4 Staff have been encouraged to comment on the system and this approach will continue with any extension implemented. It has, however, been necessary to make only minor changes and it can thus be safely concluded that the basic concept and system of Loadplan is sound, having withstood the rigours of on-site testing.

6. Extension of Loadplan

6.1 There are two reasons for recommending an extension of Loadplan:

(a) Improvement in the utilisation of the additional vehicles.

(b) Improvement in the co-ordination and use of vehicles moving between Eastern and Northern areas.

6.2 It is suggested that the following units are included in the Loadplan scheme:

	Vehicles
Newtown	1
Westley	5
Drayton	3
Oakmouth	3
Washington	7
	19

6.3 The annual cost of extending Loadplan is as follows:

Maintaining existing system		£
Loadplan officer		24,000
Car		4,600
Fax machines		250
Stationery		100
	(A)	28,950

Extending the system		£
Loadplan clerk		13,000
Fax machines		200
Stationery		100
	(B)	13,300
Plus O & M charge	(C)	14,000
A + B + C		56,250

6.4 If an improvement of £40 earnings per vehicle day (that is £8000 per vehicle year) can be achieved, the annual benefits of Loadplan would be:

(a) existing scheme £184,000;

(b) extended scheme £152,000.

7. Distribution

7.1 With the use of Loadplan, distribution of the company's products can be co-ordinated to ensure that:

(a) orders are placed on the most economic supplying unit;

(b) materials are available;

(c) vehicles are available.

7.2 In addition, changes during the working day can be coordinated via the Loadplan Officer so that vehicles are not moved to less remunerative work.

7.3 The extension of Loadplan into the Northern area creates a need to examine the shipping operations and the demand pattern at each unit. This work must be carried out prior to extending the system.

7.4 Close co-operation is necessary between the order office, the Loadplan office and the Traffic Manager. Because of this, it is suggested that the Loadplan office is permanently located at Wellington close to the order office. The link between the Traffic Manager and Loadplan Officer should be by telephone.

7.5 The report on the implications of Loadplan on the units in the extended scheme will be prepared in advance of the training and implementation of the system.

8. Conclusion

8.1 If the recommendations of this report are accepted it is suggested that the following action is taken:

(a) improvements in existing pilot scheme;

(b) change existing scheme to a permanent operation;

(c) investigate the extension into Northern area;

(d) introduce Loadplan into Northern area.

8.3 Finally, this is an excellent opportunity to express our thanks to all personnel in Eastern and Northern areas who have co-operated so willingly in the introduction and operation of Loadplan. Any benefits created by the system must be due to their efforts in ensuring that the difficulties of changing from one system to another were so easily overcome.

Bibliography

Bentley, T. J. (1992) 'Presenting Accounting information' in *IT Management Handbook*, eds. Rob Dixon and Ray Franks, Chapter 2, Butterworth-Heinemann/CIMA.

Gowers, Sir Ernest (1970) *Complete Plain Words*, Penguin.

Strunk, Williams and White E. B. (1979) *The Elements of Style*, Macmillan.

There are also a number of Internet sites that can provide further guidance, particularly on technical report writing: keyword 'Report Writing'.

Index